The Opal Within Us
Speaker Of The Souls

Understanding Animal Voices

by ROBYNN McCANN

©2010 Robynn McCann
ISBN-10: 0-9842100-0-8
ISBN-13: 978-0-9842100-0-8

Published by
ELEPHANTSDANCE PUBLISHING
P.O. Box 3239 #306
La Pine, OR 97739
Website: www.elephantsdance.org
Email: info@elephantsdance.org

Elephant Design: Joshua McCann

Cover Art: Photo of "Almost Got It All Ranch"

Editor – Linda Martin
Martin & Martin Editorial Services
P.O. Box 462, Loomis, CA 95650
Email: Linda.MartinX2@gmail.com

Graphic Designer – Bryan Rodgers
www.brodgers.net
bryan@brodgers.net

All rights reserved. No part of this book may be reproduced in any form, including Photostat, microfilm, xerography or other means, or incorporated into any information-retrieval system, electronic or mechanical, without written permission from the copyright owner.

First Edition – January 2010

CONTENTS

Preface	i
Acknowledgments	v
A Special Dedication	1
Colors of Hope	7
Stop Pacing	21
Think Not Of Yourself	29
Opal – A Story Of Acceptance	45
The Blackbird – Effortless Support	75
Blessings of Death – A Grandmother's Passing	81
The Present Isn't Always Just Now	93
All Power Comes From Within	103
Look Around!	113
Get On With Our Dreams	121
New Possibilities	131
Don't Search For What Isn't There	139
Accept Whatever May Come	145
Life Is Uncertain – Make It Wonderful!	155
Reginald: The Last Chapter	165
About The Author	179

PREFACE

Almost Got It All Ranch is the name of our home in the Sierra Foothills of Northern California, where these stories unfolded. It started out as just a family home with two children, one dog, three goats and empty pastures. Later we added pigs, sheep, more goats, horses, donkeys, llamas and cattle. The veterinarian often referred to our ranch animals as a "menagerie."

The ranch has seen hundreds of animals come and go. Most were healthy, productive breeders, and our birthing seasons occurred twice a year, with 40-60 babies each round. Watching all the babies run at one time from one end of the prairie to another was like watching a flock of birds circling to land. Many times people would stop their cars to watch the show. We had many wonderful experiences with the healthy animals that were worthy of a story, but this book is about the lessons the animals communicated to us through their illness or death, which are the most profound messages.

The ranch got its name because we took in animals that were sick, left to die or ill-treated and gave them a wonderful place to live where they would "almost have it all." We ended up with a variety of animals with a myriad of different problems. Most ranchers wouldn't give these animals a second chance. Not us, they all had the best of care and our devoted attention. They had automatic water and heat lamps in each stall, a special birthing stall. They had acres to roam, pasture grass to graze, grain and, of course, treats from the ranch's trees, almonds, figs, plums, peaches and acorns, not to mention the fresh rose petals and mulberry leaves.

This book is unique in format and structure. It doesn't read like a novel, a biography or a romance. It isn't a factual book, either. It is refreshing, I think, because the stories read like a personal journal and the story is often being told by the animals themselves. Some stories are told by me, while others include the entire family. Each chapter is a story of its own, yet when all of the stories are put together, it becomes clear we were truly blessed by the presence of all these creatures.

The stories combine various styles, including my descriptions and experiences, actual communication by the animals, communication through spirit guides and references or quotations from other material. Some of the stories include details of therapies and treatments we used with the animals and may read more like a journal than a story, others are tearful but with deep meaning and connection.

Some of the stories mention the use of Reiki, an ancient healing art using the "laying on of hands" touch healing process, and others include the use of color, during which I deviate from the story to explain the theory.

I do not consider myself a writer as we commonly think of writers or authors. My book came to be because I journaled the farm experiences as I was being taught and my own personal journey unfolded. It became evident as I shared these stories with friends and others they could feel the passion and connection, and many thought I should write them into a book to share with more people.

It's been nearly two years since all the chapters were written, including Reginald: The Last Chapter. But something was missing. What was it all of these stories about the animals had in common? What was it that made these stories deserving of being gathered together under one cover? In my struggle to finish this book, I spent a lot of time alone, meditating.

In my search for answers, I happened upon a book by Oriah Mountain Dreamer entitled "The Call." Oriah's book helped me remember who I am. I was so busy doing I forgot to just be. This book brought everything together, providing the answer to what was missing in my book: We are all here to share one thing with the world, and that is who we are.

Once we understand what our one thing is and allow it to just be, everything else falls into place. Often, this one thing we are here to share with the world is the one thing we fight with the most, the one thing we find hardest to do. If we are good at something, then it is not something we have to learn, we already know it, so it offers us nothing. As I was reading the next-to-last chapter of Oriah's book, everything came together, and, in that moment of not doing and just being I found myself and knew the one word that described who I am: Dance.

I don't mean the waltz or the tango, I mean the dance of life, the balance. I immediately knew this, too, is what all the stories had in common, what the animals were teaching me, teaching all of us – how to Dance, how to Just Be. In all their stories, no matter what illness or tragedy befell them, the common thread is, they were Just Being. They are telling us: It is what it is, don't fight it. It's all good!

In reality, the animals are the authors; I am merely the means for them to speak. They have a message to share, and when they find someone willing to listen and communicate, the animals come, ready to be heard. These stories have a very special meaning to me and my family, and I hope that you will be drawn into the stories and the journey with us.

ACKNOWLEDGMENTS

This book has been an inspiration to me and my family, with each member contributing in many ways. My husband Michael and two children, Joshua and Ahrynn, have personally cared for our animals with daily chores, assisting with birthing, caring for the sick and dying. Ahrynn has shared her communication gifts with the animals, as well. Michael has been a wonderful support emotionally, making sure I have the special time to write and work with the animals, never criticizing, judging or doubting. He shared my enthusiasm even when he didn't understand exactly how it works. He is never angered nor jealous of my late nights at the barn or lengthy meditations on the hill.

Through my grandmother's death process, she allowed me to experience death and dying in a new way that would be an important part of my work with the animals and my spiritual growth. The Spirit Guides added clarity and assisted in communication, their words and contributions are special. And, of course, the animals that have been members of our ranch family, even though not all have a story in this book, each and every one made an imprint on our lives.

A SPECIAL THANKS goes to Debra, Linda W. and Jan, who were the first three to read the early versions of this book. Because of their comments, the book was rewritten to incorporate many of their insightful suggestions.

I would also like to thank Linda M. for the endless editing and condensing of each chapter and various format suggestions, which were the perfect solution to combining the story and journal styles together.

And, thank you to Bryan for hours of graphic design, picture placements, unique layout ideas which in the end pulled everything together and made a manuscript look like a book.

A SPECIAL DEDICATION

Although this book is about animals, it would not be complete without the story of my grandmother's death. It is through her death that I was given a gift. The gift of the elephants. Her death process provided the opportunity to walk through a new door, to finally listen to that small, still voice.

When I was a child, I had dreams about elephants. I never understood the reason for the recurring dreams, but it was the same exact dream over and over. The elephants would come to my house asking for me. I hid in the closet until I thought it was safe. They found me and followed me through the field as I ran to my grandmother's house. I hid there, too. They asked for me and searched the house, so I ran again. I would wake from the dream with my heart beating fast, my palms sweaty, adrenalin rushing. I was scared. Why were elephants chasing me?

I married and had children of my own. The dreams still came. I shared this dream with my husband, knowing it was just a silly dream but not understanding why I kept having it.

When my grandmother died, THE DREAMS STOPPED! It was then and only then I realized the dreams were not to scare me. As a child, I thought I was being chased, when actually the elephants were only asking for me. When I would not answer, they had to follow me. They were persistent in their quest. It was during my grandmother's death process I accessed the Energy of the Elephants, and the dreams stopped. They no longer needed to find me, I had finally answered.

I also find it interesting it was my grandmother's house I went to hide in, and it was at my grandmother's deathbed where the elephants found me. I explain this more completely in The Blessings Of Death (Chapter 6).

DEATH IS A BLESSING. THANK YOU GRANDMA NAN FOR THE JOURNEY OF DEATH TOGETHER.

Do not stand at my grave and weep.
I am not there, I do not sleep.
I am a thousand winds that blow.
I am the diamond glints on snow.
I am the sunlight on ripened grain.
I am the gentle autumn rain.
Do not stand at my grave and cry.
I am not there, I did not die.

Mama Chia in "Sacred Journey of the Peaceful Warrior"
(Page 224) By Dan Millman

*Feel the burning desire to Live,
The flowing river of Life in our veins,
The Passion of Love in our hearts
to fuel the fire of our most sacred desires!*

by Ahrynn McCann

CHAPTER 1
COLORS OF HOPE

Once again we were at the auction, a place where buyers and sellers exchange animals. We have purchased most of our stock there, some healthy and some that could barely walk. We typically attend when it's time to purchase a buck or ram for the herd, and we usually come back with more than what we went for in the first place. This particular day was no exception.

We had a reputation with the auctioneer of accepting/purchasing animals no one else wanted. When these animals would enter the arena (in some instances, carried in), the auctioneer would start the bidding. With no bids heard, he would look at us straight on and say, "Mike, do you want it?" We couldn't refuse. Regardless of the animal's condition, we were willing to give them hope.

Well HOPE is what we got this time. A goat that couldn't walk, was carried into the arena, nearly dead. Under normal circumstances, she was a typical size goat but, given her severe malnutrition, she was frail and lifeless, maybe weighed 30 pounds. Just as she was carried into the arena, she was carried out to our trailer. We named her Hope.

On the drive home, we couldn't help but wonder how someone could ignore an animal, leave them in such ill care. Upon arriving home, we backed the trailer as close as we could to the barn so Michael wouldn't have to carry Hope so far. All the other animals knew we had a new arrival. They could smell her. Curiosity getting the best of them, the animals made their way from the field to the barn to get a closer look. Michael unlatched the back trailer gate and walked inside, and I helped him scoop up Hope into his arms. He carried her to a private stall, and laid her down in some fresh straw. Each stall had automatic water affixed to the wall, but Hope was unable to stand or walk to it, so I got a bucket of water and placed it next to her on the ground.

With Hope settled and in a comfortable place, Michael and I just sat in the stall with her for awhile, assessing her needs. It was evident she had an old jaw injury. We weren't sure if this contributed to her malnutrition or if it was just neglect. Time would tell. Her ribs were protruding, her hips were sunk in, the bones in her neck were hard and rigid, with hardly any muscle or substance. Her stomach was drawn in, but her eyes were clear and she could still hold her head up. A good sign, as inability to hold up the head is usually a sign of serious illness.

We couldn't see any other physical trauma, other than the jaw, and decided the best treatment for her now would be to just fill her up with lots of wholesome food. Even though we wanted to give her a full-course banquet of fruits, grains, nuts, tree leaves and rose petals, we knew we had to start out with just the basics – hay, and not too rich, either. We started a full spectrum of antibiotics and vitamins. We promised Hope she would never starve, would have green grass, hay, grain and a warm stall to stay in out of the rain and cold.

A few days passed with just a diet of hay. You couldn't tell Hope she had a jaw injury and couldn't eat! She had figured out how to manage. It took her longer to eat her hay than it would without the injury. You could tell she was pondering or thinking while eating, because she tipped her head from side to side as she moved the food in her mouth, using her tongue to slide the food into just the right spot to effectively chew it to perfection. We realized, with her determination, it wasn't the injury that caused her malnutrition, it was definitely neglect. How sad.

Several weeks passed and Hope was standing strong, walking with sure-footed steps. She was putting on weight and looking much better. Because Hope was so fragile and frail, we had kept her separated from the other animals. New arrivals always go through the "you're the new one" process and get butted around, just to remind them of their place. Hope was too weak to endure the welcome party.

We had back doors to each stall that opened to a corral. This was very handy during birthing season. We could keep all the animals without babies on one side of the barn and the moms with babies on the other side. We controlled which animals could go in and out. This worked perfectly for Hope. She could go into the stall and see and smell the others but go out the back to her own private yard.

Still separated from the other goats, Hope was spending more time at the fence between the corral and our backyard. The dogs became used to her presence and didn't make a fuss over her. We finally decided to open the gate and let her into the yard with us, a gesture that would normally end in disaster with most goats, as they would eat every bush to the ground. But not with Hope. She seemed to know her boundaries and was content to eat whatever was already on the ground. She sat with us in the yard, nearly climbing into our laps to eat what we had: peanuts, oranges, cookies, chips, a real garbage gut. She was starting to become a real pet. The dogs accepted Hope as one of them and actually engaged in playful antics with her. But let another goat try to come in, and the dogs would stand their ground and keep them on the other side in the prairie where they belonged!

Michael's parents travel throughout the winter and typically stay over with us for the summer months, their motorhome parked in our backyard under the mulberry trees. From this spot, they can see out into the prairie and watch the animals. As they sit in their chairs under the awning, they are greeted by the dogs and Hope, each looking for that special treat or tidbit that is so well-deserved. Hope settled into this lifestyle very easily. She enjoyed the daily attention, special treats, roaming wherever she pleased. She even played with the dogs every now and then. She stayed in the yard so much that when she had to go into the prairie and be a goat with the others, there was always a fuss stirred up — new ranking order had to be established, as if she were a new arrival.

This particular summer, Michael's parents left our place, traveled for a month and then returned. We noticed during their absence Hope had lost weight. We figured it was just because she hadn't been getting all the snacks she was used to and maybe she missed the human company. We figured with them back, Hope would put weight back on.

A few months went by and Hope wasn't putting on weight, but she still seemed fine. She socialized with the other goats, was foraging in the field and walking strong. Then, a couple weeks later, she seemed to be losing her ability to balance and didn't have her usual appetite. It was Christmas time and I was just too busy with the holiday to-do list. I didn't need a sick goat right then. But, as things would go, it never is about what I need or don't need, the animals seem to get sick when I am the busiest. So, no surprise, I guess.

It was the weekend, a beautiful spring-like day in January, and it was my turn to feed the animals. I noticed Hope was laying in a different spot in her stall than when she went to bed under the heat lamp the night before. This seemed unusual because she typically stays under the heat lamp all night. Even if we haven't turned it on yet, she stands under it and just waits until it comes on. I fed the rest of the herd first and returned to feed her and move her outside for some sunshine. I saw that she had rolled to her side, her legs stretched out straight and stiff, her eyes rolled back, her mouth open and tongue hanging. I saw her leg was shaking and trembling, so I knew she was still alive.

I quickly entered the stall, told her I was with her and held her head up to comfort her. While I was doing this, she seemed to "snap out of it." Her eyes became normal, she swallowed and closed her mouth. I rolled her up onto her belly and she held her head up on her own. I was amazed. I thought she was taking her last breath, yet a few minutes later she appeared to be just fine.

With this unusual display, I knew today was the day I must give up everything else I wanted to do and take care of Hope. There was no more delaying. Yesterday she was fine, standing on her back legs, kneeling on her front knees, eating grain and hay very vigorously. Since she had been dropping weight, I was glad to see she had an appetite. Today, she couldn't even stand on her back legs, only on her knees. So, Michael and I literally pushed, pulled and lifted her through the door to the back of the barn into the sunshine.

We both recalled how we had been here before carrying her home from the sale. It seems as though the animals we purchase from the sale in neglected condition have a tendency to easily become ill again, even after rehabilitation. Regardless of the wonderful care we give them and the healthy environment they are in, they seem to have a weakened immune system and frail physical body.

Once in the sunshine, I mixed up my special concoction, which consists of various herbs and minerals for boosting energy. To ensure she got the full dosage, I fed Hope with a turkey baster. She was thirsty, she was actually trying to suck on the plastic baster to get more faster. Once the liquids were down, it was time for some fiber made with Gerber baby rice cereal, molasses and sugar to give her something easy to digest. She started to gobble this up, too; she was hungry. She ate about one-third of the mixture and then turned her head to look at her stomach. I guess she noticed the contraction causing regurgitation, which was uncomfortable. I could see by her manners and expression she wanted to eat, yet she connected that eating made her feel bad. I decided we should feed her little bits throughout the day to keep her from being uncomfortable. She ate an orange but didn't want a banana.

With chores completed for the day, I sat in the sunshine with Hope, did some Reiki (hands-on healing energy therapy) and then asked the Universe to assist her with some color therapy. I wanted to try to send her color and see if this would help her. I always ask that this either assist in healing or in providing comfort if healing is not what is in the plan at this time.

I asked Hope if she would be willing to receive the color and use it as needed. I felt that she agreed. I also told Hope that we enjoy her being here, but if it is her time to leave, we will help make it as comfortable as possible. As I placed my hand on her side, I closed my eyes and asked the Universe to partake in this wonderful moment, to use me as a vessel and allow whatever colors were to be seen to be passed on to Hope. I waited, and nothing happened.

I began to wonder if I was going to receive any colors, what it was she needed, or had it been too long since I took the time and I couldn't see colors anymore. Then, in my frustration at the lack of results, I heard a voice, "Be still and know." I sat in a minute of meditation, repeating the words "Be still and know." Within a few moments… it started to happen.

The colors were displayed in full array. Sometimes I get a small dot of color inside another larger-shaped color with a ring of another color. This time, the entire "screen" was all one color. It was just a solid mass.

The first color was red. It was very deep and bright at the same time. It was a very intense red. I could feel the color pass through me and the warmth of my hand on Hope's side as she, too, received the color. Then came white, then a brilliant yellow and a faded orange. The orange wasn't deep or bright, almost like it had a little yellow in it, but it was still orange. Each of these colors were in full screen, they did not overlap or fade one to another. One came into view, left and the other appeared. That was it. Four colors: Red, White, Yellow and Orange.

With my eyes closed, I just sat with Hope, then I noticed a loud, annoying buzzing sound around us. I opened my eyes to see a very large fly in our space. This fly wanted to be sure I knew of its presence. There had been a little housefly on my hand the entire time I touched Hope's side meditating with the color. The larger fly returned a second time, flew close to my face and ears so I would notice it.

RED:
Red relates to our physical body, survival and our relationships; needing to overcome fear, such as of the future or death. Red energizes, increases strength. Red means you are ready to get down to business and be a leader.

WHITE:
White is Divine/Enlightenment; connecting with your higher self. White relates to helping others while looking at the larger purpose. White is cleansing and will help with clearing out negative energy. With courage and confidence, you will be able to handle the demands of the situation.

YELLOW:
Yellow reflects the intellect, intuition and self-esteem. Yellow strengthens inner power and improves the ability to make decisions and trust those decisions. Yellow says enjoy the challenge of new interests.

ORANGE:
Orange governs emotions, relationships and creativity. Orange assists in managing desires and the creativity of life forces. Orange also stimulates the appetite and reduces tiredness.

In my own thinking regarding the significance of the specific order of the colors, it would stand to reason that once Hope has energized herself with Red, has added courage and confidence through White and takes on the challenge through Yellow, the Orange brings up the rear by increasing her appetite and reducing her tiredness, which, in the end, balances the circle of the four colors.

I never saw it again throughout the entire day as I walked around the yard or each time I passed by to feed Hope. I told Hope that this fly had a message to give us and I would look it up, along with the meaning of the colors and share it with her.

That evening, as promised to Hope, I took the color and animal books off the bookcase and read the significance of the colors and their order, as well as the significance of the fly. Here is what I found.

My daughter Ahrynn was still home from school for Christmas vacation, but I had to return to work. Ahrynn made sure Hope received her fluids and rice cereal to provide the nutrition she needed without heavy digestion. She also gathered some leaves and fresh grass, put them in a bucket and Hope gobbled it all up. I didn't arrive home until 7 p.m., so I was anxious to hear how Hope progressed during the day.

As I drove past the barn, I could see the light in Hope's stall, so I knew she was still with us. As I walked in the house, I said, "I see Hope is still here." Michael said yes, but he wasn't sure for how long. He and Ahrynn said Hope didn't do as well today as yesterday. She wasn't able to get out of the stall, she couldn't stand on any legs at all. Ahrynn said she had to scoot her to the doorway so she could at least look out at the sunshine. It is a southern exposure, a sunny day, so she was able to see and feel some warm rays. I did a few things in the house before changing and going down to see her.

As I went into the stall, Hope perked up, looked well, her eyes were clear, she was alert and she had hay in her mouth. I told her she looked good and that I had a treat for her. I showed her a mandarin orange, one of her favorite foods. I could hardly get it peeled, she was so anxious for a bite. I gave her some peeling and continued to peel faster and faster. She ate the entire orange. I moved the hay and separated it so she could get to the tender, loose flakes inside without as much effort.

Hope was laying along the wall of the stall under the heat lamp; she enjoyed her heat lamp. As I sat next to her, I put my arm over her shoulders and along her side and began to rub her and talk to her. I noticed she appeared a lot thinner than just 36 hours ago. She was unable to stand or even roll from side to side. She was weak, but very alert and attentive. As I sat with her, I asked her if she had decided to stay or go. I told her how special she was, she was the only goat the dogs would let into the yard, but if she was ready to go, that was okay. She has a journey and a purpose, and if that has been completed, then it was time to let go of her physical body and move on.

This would be the hardest part, the letting go, but I would do what I could to help. I sat for awhile longer with her just being in her presence. Then I felt her desire to let go and not stay. I told her I would call in the assistance of the Universe. I surrounded us with white light and asked for the spirits and guides to join us, including the Reiki and elephant energy. As I settled in for the next step, I told the Universe that I was grounded, my bottom was sitting on the dirt of the stall floor, my feet were resting on the dirt as well. I was rooted in Mother Earth and would like to make myself available as a vessel to assist this animal's

FLY:
Depending on the weather, warm or cold, the fly emerges anywhere from one week to two months. Extremes in weather do not typically last long, which can relate to our extreme situations being short in duration. It is possible for us to remain stable during these extreme times until we, too, can emerge.

Most flying insects have more than one pair of wings. Flies only have one pair specially designed to keep them stable and balanced in flight. This signifies that, even though things around us seem impossible or difficult, we will remain balanced while maneuvering into position.

Compared to its small body, a fly's metallic eyes are very large. This signifies the ability to see the color of life regardless of what the situation is.

Putting this all together, I believe the fly was telling us Hope's unhealthy situation would not last long and, even though she couldn't stand or balance, she should not second-guess it. When Hope thinks she wants to stand or move, she should take action and she will be more balanced and stable than she may believe possible. She will see all the possibilities.

soul in leaving this earth plane as peacefully as possible. I pulled Hope's neck around, raised my leg and put her head over my leg to rest upon it and cradled her head in my other arm. She was snug and comfortable.

I told Hope I would call upon my totem, the elephants, to come and provide her with comfort and peace for passing. I told her they would vibrate with us. I began the deep vibrational tone for the elephants. The vibration is not of my own. It is deep, penetrating and very soothing. When the elephant's spirit is present, the vibration is felt in the depths, in the roots of my teeth, in the bone of my jaw and the soles of my feet. It is like no other feeling.

As I vibrated with the elephants, I could feel their energy pass through me to Hope. My arm was cradling her head, the other arm across her shoulders and touching her abdomen on the other side. As we vibrated, I could feel her entire body relax. Her breathing was slower, the ribs moved in and out less often, her movements were slowing. I rocked with her like a mother would with a child to help soothe and comfort her. I assured Hope that it was almost over.

021

As I vibrated, I watched the hair on the back of her neck and behind her eyes move. It moved like grass swaying in the wind. I knew she was still with us. I thought she had stopped breathing, so I lifted her head from my arm to look at her eyes. They were not clear, rather they were glazed over as if in a trance, fixed in another place. I thought maybe she was in transition, seeing what was ahead of her yet still here. I checked her gums, lips and teeth, and they were very cold, ice cold, yet she was still breathing, faintly. I put her head back into my arms and continued with the vibration of the elephants.

As I glanced toward the stall door, I noticed that 021 (one of the other goats) had been standing in front of the door to the stall the entire time on the outside looking in. I told Hope that 021 was there, that she was here to assist and give comfort, to let her know that all is well and she isn't alone in this process, that the other goats were aware of her departure. Then, 021 turned her head, and in the dark of the night in the glow of the heat lamp, she tipped her head and her eye met mine. It wasn't the usual glance of one to another. I saw through her eye to her soul. One of the books in my library said that the way to the soul of an animal is through its eyes. I saw into 021's soul and, as we shared this moment, 021 said, *"You are so compassionate; we are all grateful for the love and compassion you show us each day."* Then I heard Precious (the sheep who had died earlier this year who I sat with in the same way while she was dying) say, *"Tell Hope I will be here to meet her, she won't be alone."* So I did just that. I told Hope that Precious was waiting, and I thanked 021 for her thoughts and her support.

Hope was still in a calm, almost hypnotic state. I told her it was time for me to leave. I know that animals (even humans) do not like to pass until they are alone. I felt at peace. I felt as though the Universe with the guides and spirits and elephants had provided support and assistance and she was at peace. All was in order. As I moved her head off my lap, Hope looked up at me and, for a split second, her eyes became clear, her face became bright as if to say thank you for being with me. Then she bowed her head and rested her forehead under the heat lamp against the wall. As I got up to leave, she wouldn't look at me. I knew she was going to be gone soon.

When I arrived at the house, I told the family Hope would be gone soon. It was amazing to me how an animal could be so bright, alert and eating oranges and, within an hour, be close to death without a fight, peaceful, content and ready to pass. Some may say or think, "What about the colors the day before? Weren't the colors suggesting she was going to be strong, had future plans, increased appetite, etc?" I have learned that animals have messages for us. Sometimes the Universe, through whatever means, will facilitate an animal's healing or comfort. Other times it is just not meant to be. And sometimes the message is intended for us, not them. I have read and believe **every creature mirrors the magnificence of our own soul.** An animal can mirror different things for different people. What Hope mirrored for me is different than what she mirrored for Ahrynn. One animal, same soul, can mirror according to our individual needs.

As I went to bed that night, I sent Hope love and peace. I knew she would be gone in the morning and in a better place, with Precious. When we awoke, Michael asked if I was going to the barn to check on Hope. I said no, I would rather remember her from my experience last night and would he mind checking on her. I saw him before leaving for work, and he said Hope had died. But she was warm when she died because she was still under the heat lamp. I am certain she died shortly after I left her the night before.

Hope

Throughout the day, I teared up. Not because of the loss, even though I will miss her, but because of the opportunity she provided for me to learn and experience one more time the strength and power of the Universe. Hope provided me the opportunity, in her death, to call upon the Universe, the elephants, the guides, to reinforce that this higher energy is there for us, we just have to ask and we shall receive -- courage, faith, hope, compassion, patience, love, understanding or whatever we need at that moment in our journey. I realized Hope had waited to die until I had made the time to sit with her. I was thinking she was in need of universal assistance, and all the while she was trying to give me a message.

I alluded to it earlier. The colors we saw the day before weren't for her, they were for me. As I realized this, I remembered a statement by Ted Andrews, author of *Animal Wise*, who said, "Through sacred silence, we experience the wonders and beauty of animals more intimately, and we begin to realize that every creature mirrors the magnificence of our own soul." Hope was waiting for me so she could mirror to me these very colors.

As I look back through the meaning of this, each color was significant to my present life. The day before, I asked the Universe to provide the colors to comfort Hope, to heal Hope or provide whatever was necessary for her. Little did I realize that this message was intended for me -- another lesson on being open to the information or message provided. Through Hope, I received this message loud and clear. Once delivered, she knew she could pass, and through our experience of death together, I would see clearly the reflection in the mirror.

My tears were also a thank you to Hope for reminding me I must experience the benefits and joy of this universal energy more often. I get so caught up in work and family that I lose sight of my journey. It is through time spent with the Universe I receive strength, encouragement and instruction. The times that I have allowed myself to be with the animals, through saving a dying one or being with one to comfort through death, I have been moved into a new level of awareness about myself and my journey. I need to spend more time here, in this space, in this awareness.

Thank you for THE COLORS OF HOPE… you will be missed.

*Give yourself the power to be an open vessel
for the universe to fill your mind, body, spirit,
heart and soul, with the greatest gift ever given…
The Love for and of yourself.*
by Ahrynn McCann

CHAPTER 2

STOP PACING
Focus And Get On With Your Business

I was driving home from the store, the radio on smooth jazz, my mind empty, no agenda, no "to-do list," when I heard Pepper, my German shorthair dog, chime in. *"I have to go in order to help you. IT'S TIME. Time for me to go and time for you to start writing. My pacing is to let you know you are distracted, not focused. You need to stop going in circles, lost with no direction."*

Let me tell you what led up to this moment.

In October, Jack and Carol, my in-laws, were getting ready to leave on their southward journey for the winter months. Pepper had been taking note they were going away, things getting packed up, change of schedule, the usual things that signal to animals their friends are leaving for awhile. I noticed Pepper was acting differently. She was nearly seventeen years old, and for the past two years we had wondered how she made it through another season. I had never been able to "communicate" with Pepper. I understand sometimes we are too close to our own animals and seem to have a "block" when it comes to communicating; however, I sensed she wanted to say something. The only way I could figure to let her speak her voice was to ask a spirit guide for assistance.

As Pepper laid on the cool green grass shaded by the large mulberry tree, the spirit guide, Serena, began to speak. I just listened as the guide said Pepper had a wonderful life with us. She had a wonderful home, lots of love, many other animals as friends and we have taught her many things. She was tired of hurting and was ready to go (not necessarily today, but the time was at hand).

I asked if she wanted the vet to assist with her passing and, if so, if she wanted to be taken to the vet or stay at home. Serena said no, Pepper wanted to go naturally, she did not want to be euthanized. Serena said, *"She wants you to help her go, she wants to be in your arms."*

Pepper was sacrificing herself two-fold. First, she would let me know when it was time, providing me with the confidence of knowing I had communicated with her. Second, she would be allowing me to call upon the elephants (my totem animal) in order to assist with her passing and experience another connection with these spirited animals to help me with my own journey. You see, the only way I can practice calling the elephants is when an animal or person is nearing death and needs to go peacefully. The experience is like no other -- so empowering. Pepper said she was willing to be part of my journey.

I waited for the day when Pepper would tell me it was time for her to go. Some days I would lay with her and try to communicate, but nothing, just an empty void. Some days I would look at her and say, "Is today the day?" No change in expression and no communication, so I just moved on, keeping myself occupied with other things, knowing I wouldn't have to help her pass this day and she would be with us longer.

Time had passed after Pepper's communication through Serena, and she had become more blind and deaf. At first she was blind only at night; by day she could navigate her way through an obstacle course. She could only hear a high-pitched whistle or, in my case, since I couldn't whistle, I clapped my hands and that seemed to work. She ate twice the amount the other dogs got and still looked for leftovers from them. She ran, was able to get up and down and "whoo" (Pepper didn't bark, she whoo-whooed). She was excited to take the walk across the property from the house to the shop and would leap and run all the way. You would not know this dog was seventeen and ready to leave this place.

Over the past few months, Pepper had been refusing her medication. She was on a prescription for bladder control. It didn't matter how I disguised it -- in hot dogs, cream cheese, peanut butter -- she managed to spit it out. I decided the medicine must be affecting her in other ways I was not aware of, so I stopped giving it to her and we just dealt with the mess in the laundry room. We figured when she was gone, we'd install new carpet; until then, let it be. Pepper had started having mini strokes or seizures, but I believe they were related to the medication. On two occasions, I was there during the seizure, held her and talked to her until it was over. When she came back into consciousness, she was glad to see me and be in my arms.

As time went on, Pepper seemed to get worse. When we let her outside during daylight hours, she would go in circles, with no idea where the front or back of the yard was. She would walk up and down the driveway and around the house for hours without stopping. When she was inside the house, she would walk in circles in the laundry room, run into the glass sliding door as if she didn't know it was there. She would run into the washing machine and the walls. I had never seen her like this. We would bring her down into the family room while we watched TV, and for hours she would walk in circles, run into things, and just have no clue where she wanted to go. She must have put miles on each day and didn't go anywhere. I began to think she had Alzheimer's because she would have some days where she knew exactly where she was and other days when it was just as I described.

These events led to that day when I was driving and Pepper "chimed in" with her message. I responded by acknowledging to her I understood and would help her go so she could help me write, and I would be honored to know she was with me in spirit, a guiding force behind the journey. SHE STOPPED PACING.

Tears welled up in my eyes after I had heard the message from Pepper. I knew what she was talking about. Pepper was telling me I had put off changes in my own life long enough. I needed to STOP GOING IN CIRCLES and just do it! I also had tears because I realized the first part of what she said she would do for me had come to pass just then. She had communicated with me it was time to go, and I heard her. (Now all that was left was for me to help her pass.)

I thanked Pepper for the message and told her I would do as she had instructed me. I felt a release of guilt and pressure, almost as if I had been caught stalling and had to fess up. Pepper knew I, too, was pacing, unsettled, doing everything else except what I was supposed to be doing (starting my journey writing this book). I felt very distracted. I wouldn't sit down and write or read or do something related to my new journey until this or that was done. I knew she was right because I was feeling all knotted up inside. But my answer was to do more "ticky-tacky things," things that were meaningless and occupied my day but didn't amount to anything. Pepper needed to get my attention, and she did by taking it upon herself to start acting disoriented.

I began writing for the first time in months, and it was all because of a dog who was insistently pacing, without end, until I responded, and then she stopped pacing.

Animals are here to assist us with our journeys. They are present in the now. They only focus on *right now*, not yesterday, not tomorrow, and not an hour ago. They can assist us through a divorce, an illness or even a death and be right there for the sorrow or emptiness when a child grows up and moves out or a change in jobs creates a move. Because they are so present, they offer us the answer for each moment; we just have to pay attention and "get the message." Once we have gotten the message and act on it, things change.

With the first part of Pepper's Sacrifice — communicating with me — completed, all that was left was the second part – to help her pass.

It was January 20, 2004. I had been spending an enormous amount of time at the barn with Opal (a baby goat) and was not spending any time with Pepper. During the winter, Pepper (as well as the other dogs) stayed at the barn in the birthing stall. It was constructed with new moms in mind. Secluded from the other stalls, it is fully enclosed to protect them from the cold and rain and has two windows, one on each side, with slats that open so the mamas get fresh air and can see out. Wood shavings on the floor provide comfort, and there is an automatic waterer affixed to the wall and a heat lamp for warmth. Between this stall and the area we use to store our supplies, there is a half wall that holds a microwave for warming bottles, a table for preparing special diets and a radio to provide music. This arrangement gives us a chance to be with the mamas without actually being in their stall. The animals seemed to like the arrangement, as they were able to bond with their babies there for a few days before joining the rest of the herd. When not occupied by mama goats, it doubled as an upscale dog house!

For five days after Opal's birth, Pepper didn't get her usual attention. In the morning there was only enough time to give Pepper a pat on the head and a quick hug. At night, she was always asleep and I didn't want to wake her. Tonight, after Opal's therapy, I decided to spend some special time with Pepper in the barn.

I opened the latched door to her stall and sat on the floor under the heat lamp with Pepper laying in my lap and my arms around her. We snoodled and loved under the warmth of the heat lamp. I thanked her for being here, for being who she was and for the joy she brought us. I apologized for not spending time with her. I told her about Opal and knew she understood. I told her I knew she had told me it was time for her to go and that possibly I was ignoring her because I wasn't quite ready for her to go. By not paying attention to her, I didn't have to address the issue at hand. So, tonight I was here to help her pass on.

I told Pepper it was okay, this is what she had wanted and I would ask the Universe to be with us in this transition. I told her it would be quiet and effortless, the Universe would provide the strength to let go and release. I asked for the beings to assist, the Universe, Mother Earth and, of course, the elephants.

I began with the energy of the elephants and just held Pepper in my lap. After a little while, she began to shake and have muscle contractions like she was having small seizures, but they were controlled and rhythmic. Even with these physical changes, she was calm and seemed as if she was relaxed and working with the Universe on her departure. Then, all of a sudden, she jumped up quicker than I have ever seen her get up and ran, didn't walk, over to the water trough to get a very long drink. After her drink, she immediately returned to me, sat in my lap, my arms once again wrapped around her, and we picked up where we had left off. She twitched, she sighed, she had muscle contractions again. I told her it was okay, she was doing so well, let go and release.

I asked her heart and lungs and other organs to slow in their work as Pepper prepared to leave us. Then, as all seemed to be working for this cause, the same thing happened again. She sprang up, ran over to the water trough and, instead of coming back to me, darted out the doggy door to the outside.

I did not follow her. She returned after a few minutes and sat in my lap. I thought this was so strange. I asked the Universe to provide me with some assistance as to what this meant. I did not know what to do, to continue with the process of assisting her to go or to let her be. I thought if she got up one more time for a drink, she was to stay. In times past, if I went to the barn to sit with Pepper just to be with her, she never jumped up to get a drink. This was definitely unusual behavior for her.

We tried a third time -- energy of the elephants, Mother Earth and relaxing to let things be as they should. Once again, she got up and immediately went for the water trough. This time when she returned, I told her it must not be time and we would wait for another day when she was ready. I sat with her just visiting, no energy work, just being with her. It was a wonderful time.

I came up to the house and told my husband about the evening's events. We both noticed in the following days Pepper was more alert, had bouncy energy and was more aware of her surroundings and full of life than she had been in the past two years. My husband suggested whatever took place at the barn that night must have been very powerful, even if I didn't think it went like I had thought it should.

It is February 6, 2004, and Pepper is still with us. She has not let me know it should be any different than any other day. She whoo-whoos every morning, she jumps, she runs, she plays, she is so happy. She puts her ears up a lot, she is full of love and vigor.

I do not know what to think of this. Why is she still here? Even though she said it was time to go so she could help me write my book, maybe in her perspective "now" means not years but it doesn't necessarily mean today, either. I will keep an open mind so I may know when "now" truly means today so I will be prepared to assist once again. Until then, we are enjoying every day Pepper chooses to remain a part of this family. I love you Pepper!

*We are all given the gift and ability to teach others,
it is how we honor and create moments of enlightenment
that allows the gift of our souls to do the teaching
instead of our minds.*
>> **by Ahrynn McCann**

CHAPTER 3
THINK NOT OF YOURSELF

It was 1:30 in the morning as we drove into the yard with an empty trailer, empty halter and lead rope. Perdu had been euthanized.

Perdu's life with us began a couple years earlier when we purchased him from the nearby livestock auction. My husband, Michael, and I went that day to purchase a billy goat for our girls (ewes). We were early to the sale and decided to take a preview look at the animals waiting in the holding pens in the stockyard. We stood on the bottom rail of the fence to be taller and see across all the pens. From this vantage point, Michael saw a head and neck extending well above the pen, capturing his interest.

We stepped down off the wooden rail fence and made our way through the maze of gates, chutes and channels to finally get to the pen. We saw a beautiful white llama with brown patches near his hind end. Michael slid the wooden latch to the side and opened the stall gate to enter into the small space, which was just a holding stall with dirt floor and wooden sides about four feet tall.

The llama didn't spit, didn't kick. He wasn't real keen on Michael being in there, but nonetheless he tolerated the intrusion. Michael thought we needed to buy him. I told him we had four llamas already and didn't need anymore. As we left the stall, Michael gave me that pouty look with a big rolled-up lip and said, "He wants to come with us" (usually I am the one who says this, so for Michael to say it was something to take notice of).

Time was nearing for the sale to start. We entered the arena and sat in the front-row seats typically reserved for the serious buyers. The seats were old, red, highback chairs with torn and cracked naugahyde cushions and armrests. There was a wall of chainlink fencing in front of us. The other seats were backless, hard benches for the not-so-serious buyers. When the llama came through the auction door, Michael nudged my arm off the armrest, making sure I took notice he was in the arena and up for bid. Michael leaned over and whispered for me to bid on him, if I wanted him. I told Michael I didn't want him and didn't intend to bid.

Michael couldn't shake the thought he had earlier in the stall with the llama that he wanted to come home with us, so Michael nodded and was now in the bidding. As the bidders kept upping the ante, Michael looked at me as if to get a glance of approval. He bid some more and, with persistence, was the high bidder. Michael had his llama.

We didn't know anything about this llama -- if he was halter-broke, if he would load in a trailer – and, of course, the animals were already anxious, as they went through a major ordeal just being at the sale. To our surprise, he loaded in our trailer without hesitation and, with the door latched, we headed for home.

He was sold to us without a name, so "Perdu" was what we called him. As with all new arrivals, we kept him by himself for a few days to allow him time to acclimate to his new home, the smells of the other animals and us. As we watched him for the first day, we noticed he had a difficult time urinating. He seemed a bit swollen and his rear legs were blackened with a tar-like substance. We called the veterinarian and scheduled the first available appointment.

As soon as she drove up, Perdu knew the vet wasn't just another visitor. He knew something was up. She gave him a quick look-over and then administered a sedative so we could get a better look. Not knowing any history for him, she chose to be a little cautious on the initial dosage. The first dose was too little, he fought and fought to not give into the effects of the drug. He just refused to get sleepy and kept standing. A second dose was given and that did the trick. He wobbled, weakened at the knees and had that look of "nothing matters anymore."

Once Perdu was down, Michael and I helped to hold him in various positions so the vet could see better. It wasn't a good sight. Poor Perdu had a nasty infection. His sheath was nearly closed shut and he had been urinating inside the sheath. The blackened sticky stuff on his legs was from the urine constantly dripping with infection and then getting dirty as he walked and lay down. Somebody had ignored this lovely animal and took him to the sale so as to not have to put any money into him or care about his well-being. It is so shameful, so sad that people treat animals with so little love and compassion.

The doctor first made an opening in the sheath to relieve the pressure and clean out all the pus and infection. The area was cleaned and prepared for surgery. The skin around the sheath was so badly infected and raw it wasn't a good prospect for repair, and there wasn't much else to work with. She opted to insert a temporary drain tube to allow the urine to escape from the sheath while giving the skin time to heal. But what to use for a drain tube in this location? After a lengthy discussion of possible options, it was determined the casing of a syringe tube, cut down in size, inserted and stitched to the skin around the opening would be the best solution. Michael drilled holes in the capsule to give the needle and surgery thread a place to go through. It worked. The vet inserted the tube, drew the needle and thread through the skin, through the tube, around to the other hole, through the hole, through the skin and out the other side. She repeated this all the way around. With surgery completed, we gave Perdu a dose of antibiotics and waited for him to wake up.

The doctor hoped this would hold long enough for his skin to heal so we wouldn't have to do another surgery. Not knowing where he came from or what conditions he was living in, we didn't have a history to go from. All we knew is we were glad he came to our place, where he would certainly have a comfortable life. I told the doctor it wasn't in our plans to purchase a llama that day, we were looking for a billy goat and Michael just felt that Perdu wanted to come home with us. She said he knew he needed help and that you were just the family to do it. Looking back now, we know why Perdu was uncomfortable with Michael being in the stall; he was so infected and in such pain that having anyone near and petting him was just too sensitive.

Michael and I had to give Perdu penicillin for the next several days. We kept him in an area where it would be easy to catch him each evening for his shot. He was so good. He knew what we were going to do but didn't fuss. He never spit or kicked, as llamas often do when stressed. He was so gentle. He knew we were helping him and all would be fine.

After his treatments were finished, we let Perdu out with the other llamas. What a happy day that was for all of them. We continued to watch Perdu every day. Part of his recovery plan was to be sure he was urinating outside the sheath. That required that we look to see if he was urinating in a steady stream. Steady stream was good, dripping not so good.

One day we noticed the tube as dangling, it had come loose and was no longer inserted. I called the doctor and she said it would eventually fall all the way off, no need to catch him and remove it. She told us to just continue watching him to make sure he was always urinating a steady stream. Not too long after this, Perdu was back to just dripping. Another call to the vet.

In drove a white truck with chrome door latches on the sides and drawers that slid out from the back. Once again, Perdu knew she wasn't just a visitor. Already haltered and tied to a tree, Perdu saw the vet get out of the truck, step into her boots and coveralls, walk to the back of the truck, open up all those doors and drawers, fill her basket with goodies -- needles, syringes, antibiotics, antiseptics suturing devices, gauze and gloves – and make her way toward us.

Perdu's eyes changed from anxious to nervous, but that didn't keep him from being calm and cooperative. He knew she was there for him and the things she was going to do, although uncomfortable at first, would make him feel better soon. This time, we knew exactly how much sedative to give him. The needle, the poke, that look of nothing mattered, wobbly knees and down he went. It wasn't good this time, either. Back to square one, with a twist.

The skin was so raw and sore the vet wouldn't be able to use it for suturing. She opted to cut away the skin around the sheath opening and pull or roll skin from inside to the outside to create a new, healthy opening. Another tube was inserted like before. We had hopes that this would work since he did not have the infection like the first time. Several days of antibiotics were again given to be sure.

Perdu was so good about the daily routine of shots. Finished with treatments, he was once again let out to pasture with the other llamas. We continued to duck and check him every chance we got. Whenever we would happen to notice him urinating, we stopped to watch. Every family member was told to be on the lookout for Perdu and report on his status!

It had been quite some time since the surgeries. Perdu had been without another incident, but still we always checked. The llamas and goats had an opportunity to go to another home for spring pasture, consisting of acres of open fields, a running creek, blackberry bushes, and a variety of foliage trees providing a banquet feast. All the walking kept them in great physical shape.

The spring pasture was not our own property. It was a few miles away. We weren't used to having our animals away, not being able to see them every day or walk out into the pasture to spend time with them, and it left an empty feeling. Every other day, one or more of us would drive out to the spring pasture just to check on everyone. Of course, the dogs had to go along for a swim in the creek. Upon our arrival, the llamas and several of the goats would always come down from where they were to see us and check for the goodies we brought. Although they didn't need it, some days we would bring hay or grain just for some variety and to get them used to coming down to us for when we would want to load them to go home again.

Perdu was always the first to arrive. He would see us drive up and, before we could out of the vehicle, open the gate, let the dogs in and put hay on the ground, he was there. He was fast and always ran full-steam. It is so fun to watch llamas run, their head down, moving from side to side, pointing them in the direction to go. When Perdu would get down to where we were, we made sure one of us was able to get a good look at his sheath. If that meant getting down on our hands and knees to see his underside, that's what we did. It was always wonderful when the inspection indicated everything was working perfectly, no swelling, no infection.

We spring-pastured the animals for two seasons. Usually the animals came back to our property in the fall and winter, but this year was different. We were moving fences and changing out irrigation lines, so we left them there for the winter. With all our chores completed, the animals were returning home in February and would spend the summer with us. We were all very excited to bring them home.

On moving day, I was unable to go along, so Michael took his mom and dad with him. They loaded some hay and grain, along with some makeshift panels to create a temporary catch-pen for easier loading into the trailer. The first day was the llamas, second day would be the goats and sheep. Michael called me at work as soon as he got the llamas home and said Perdu was in bad shape and I needed to call the vet. He thought it was strange because he had just been out to the pasture four days earlier to feed and, as usual, Perdu was the first one down and looked fine. How could something go wrong so quickly and so long after he had been well?

Michael said this time when he pulled into the field, Perdu was the last one down for feed, he didn't want to walk down the hill and cross the creek. Michael had to actually cross the creek and get behind him to work his way down the field. He knew then something wasn't right.

When I got home, we put Perdu in the barn area by himself. We both noticed fluid building up on the inside of his front legs under his chest. He never had that before, so we realized there was more going on than expected. I called the vet that evening and left a message about the fluid retention in case that might change her general prognosis. Wednesday morning the vet returned my call and said the best she could fit in for a visit was on Friday afternoon. All of us assumed Perdu was having a recurrence of his previous illness and getting him started on penicillin right away would help until she could get here. She had us start him on 20cc of penicillin per day, injecting 10 on each side. He was so good once again, never flinched. We didn't even need to restrain or hold him, just give him the shots and be done with it. He was drinking a ton of water, nibbling at hay and grass. He didn't want any grain, bananas, pineapple, no treats, but his spirits were good. He spent most of his time laying down, but would get up and walk around a little. We could tell he was uncomfortable, as he drew his hips inward and walked with great pain. You could see it in his eyes.

Michael and I had planned a trip to Arizona, but with Perdu in this condition, there was no way we would leave him unattended, so I stayed behind. I gave him his shots the next day and the following day the vet was to arrive. I waited as long as I could on Friday to give him his shot as I figured, if the vet was coming, we could give him the penicillin while he was sedated and he wouldn't have to have another stick of the needle.

Each day, and several times a day, I went out and sat with Perdu in his pasture. At times I would lean my head against his shoulder. I kissed his nose and the soft side of his cheeks. These were special moments. We watched the clouds, we watched the other animals in the pasture, we snuggled, and I just loved him. I was his company.

My daughter walked by one Friday afternoon while I was laying with Perdu and looked surprised. She commented on how quiet and content he was to have me laying next to him. Usually llamas will get up as soon as you approach them too closely. I got up and said, "Oh, not only will he let me lay here next to him, but look what else he lets me do." Then I showed her how I cradle his neck and head in my chest and kiss him all over, and he hums to me while I rub his eyes and the top of his head. She couldn't believe he was that docile.

It was getting later in the day, the sun was dipping behind the trees on the horizon and the vet hadn't arrived yet, so I asked Ahrynn to help me give Perdu his shot. She stood next to him, held his halter, and knowing he was uncomfortable, asked if he was going to spit at her or jump up when I poked him. I said no, he doesn't feel well enough. I gave him his shot while he lay down. I couldn't believe it, he didn't even try to get up. It was too easy. He was very patient and knew it had to be done. We stayed with him awhile longer and then went to the house.

The vet called and wanted to know if I had lights so we could see to do the evaluation and possible surgery. I said yes. Then she asked me how he was. I told her that Wednesday he was urinating a little stream, by Thursday it was only dripping and by today, Friday, there was nothing. He would stand up to urinate and try so hard, but nothing. She was very concerned and said she was on her way.

We readied the barn with floodlights and extension cords. We have lights at the barn, but Perdu was in the grassy area up from the barn. I thought it would be better to work up there, more room, open space and, with all of us around, I didn't want him feeling crowded. So the floodlights were extended up to where Perdu was. When the vet arrived, Perdu didn't even try to get up. He knew who she was and why she was there. Despite his anxiety and discomfort, once again he cooperated with every request. He stood so she could evaluate him, his head held high and strong. Looking at him, you wouldn't know he was ill or in discomfort, he just looked like a healthy llama laying down. He "hummed" to the other llamas and me (sign of contentment), was alert, wasn't underweight, just an all-around strong llama with a large, bloated abdomen. In all his pain, he never tried to spit or kick anyone. He welcomed the company and companionship of us around. He was willing to share his love.

The vet and I discussed the events of the week, the timing of when we think he started getting ill. She noticed he did not have the tar-like stains on his legs like before. The swelling and fluid under his chest was not like before, either. She gave him the sedation and we watched and waited for him to sink into that bliss state. As usual, he fought it. We watched him try to lay down but not give into the drug. It was like watching a drunk person try to walk. The lights were bright, so once he gave in and was down, the vet put a coat under his head and over his eyes so he was more comfortable. I stayed up at his neck just in case he should get scared or try to get up. Ahrynn watched the doctor as she started her evaluation.

Perdu didn't have an infection in the sheath as before. He was very swollen, and the opening to the sheath was nearly closed shut. She needed to do a rectal exam, so on went the gloves. She could feel the bladder was very full and enlarged but intact. I told her I hadn't seen any fresh feces in the barn area, so I couldn't tell her the last time he moved his bowels. She confirmed that his bowels were completely empty. I told her he had only been snacking these last few days, nibbling at the hay and grass but not aggressively eating. He was, however, drinking at least one bucket of water a day, which in his situation only added to the discomfort of not being able to urinate.

The vet decided to do an ultrasound to see if she could get any more definitive information. She saw the bladder and the urethra but couldn't find the penis. The bladder was very large and the urethra appeared to have a blockage or a tear. She couldn't tell which it was, but it was definitely something.

Based on the results of the ultrasound, her initial rectal exam and the fluid retention in the legs under the chest, she believed he had edema from leakage of urine out of the urethra into the body cavity. Since there wasn't any infection, we had three options: euthanasia, a trip to Davis for emergency surgery, or an attempt at a field surgery here and now. The field surgery would only be a temporary fix and the risk of infection was very high. The procedure would have to be repeated every three months, with very strict caregiver commitment. The surgery at Davis would provide a more advanced diagnosis with a sterile environment, which would reduce the risk of infection. After thoroughly discussing all options in detail, I decided to make the trip to Davis. If euthanasia ended up being the only way to go, at least we would have investigated the options further and given Perdu the best chance to be healed.

As the vet put her things away in the truck, Perdu was still sedated, and we talked a little more about him. Our mutual concern was whether or not Perdu would get better and stay better. When we purchased him, he had a urinary infection. He'd been better for a year or two and now this, which was different but still urinary related. She said this type of infection in a llama is very rare, not much is known about it. Although in some areas llamas are very similar to goats, this is not that similar. If surgery worked for Perdu (the success rate for these types of surgery on llamas is not very high), he would most likely have the same or related problem again. Is it fair to ask him to go through this so we can have him as part of our family? When is enough, enough?

That's when we let the animal decide. If we truly listen with our heart and soul, they will tell us. The vet commented that Perdu was very fortunate to come here. Had we not purchased him, he may not have ever received any treatment and lived a very painful life as short as it may have been. She wrote up the referral sheet with detailed information from her examination for me to take to Davis. While I waited for the orders, I had a moment to reflect:

I am not willing to keep an animal alive for me. Animals have a journey and a purpose, too. They are so attentive to us, so in-tune with our emotions, they teach us. We must be willing to listen, observe and see what they have to tell. When it is time for an animal to go, it's time to go, and they will let you know.

As I looked back on the events that took place, the time I spent with Perdu in the field the three days waiting for the vet were very special times. He was so content, even though in great pain. He let me share his love, he let me lay with him and hold him. I felt so connected to him. I didn't try to communicate with him and ask him what he wanted, at that time I didn't know the extent of his illness. I assumed it would be as simple as before, do the surgery, the antibiotics and we're done. I wasn't thinking that these were the last few days of his life. I was in the moment with him, pure love being exchanged between us. At one time on Friday, I thought I would see what color I might be able to send him, and no more did I start the thought than I stopped, deciding instead to just be present with him. Now I know that he knew it was his time, that things weren't going to get fixed, and he showed me to just love, be present and enjoy our time together, all will be fine. His eyes were so loving, so gentle, so kind. He didn't have a care in the world. He knew, but I didn't, that things would be over soon, his pain would be gone and he would be in a better place.

As the vet left, I noticed Perdu was starting to come out of his sedation. His ears were up, his head was tilted off the ground a little, and he was rolling his eyes around. I told him we were going to another place to see if we could get him better and that I would come back in a little while to load him in the trailer when he was more sure-footed. I went to the house, called the Davis facility and advised them of my arrival. I spoke to the doctor on duty and gave him all the information from the exam and discussed what our intentions were. Figuring it could be a long evening, Ahrynn and I ate some dinner before loading Perdu and making the trip to Davis.

With Ahrynn in the truck and Perdu in the trailer, we started off through town. We had to stop for gas. As we got out of the truck, Perdu had his head out the window of the trailer. All you could see was three-quarters of his neck and his head. His ears perked up, he was interested in the bright lights and city stuff. One of the customers at the station asked what kind of animal he was and, of course, I told him a llama. I offered for him to bring his wife over to pet him, he thanked me but never came to see Perdu. I wish I had my camera, a llama in a horse trailer with his head outside the window is picture-perfect. He stayed that way for quite some time while we drove down the road. As I think back now, I believe he was saying his goodbyes, he was taking in all the smells of his environment and enjoying his last few hours.

We arrived at Davis at 9:45 in the evening on February 24th. Perdu unloaded from the trailer perfectly. He walked right into the big, bright open space of the clinic. Big roll-up warehouse doors, squeeze chutes with bright-blue padding, hardware hanging from the racks above, machines everywhere, strange people, concrete floors, he never stopped or refused. He knew this was the last stop. Once again he was prodded and poked. His neck was shaved to allow for drawing blood. He didn't mind the sound of the shaver, a handheld, standard barber shaver used on men's haircuts. He leaned his head into my shoulder.

Perdu was stuck inside the squeeze chute, bars on all sides. He was nervous and afraid, but so cooperative. The attendants weren't able to hit the vein on that side, so they switched to the other and shaved once again. Perdu was very alert, not missing a thing. He looked at everything all around him, he looked at the people. I could see something different in his eyes this time. At home he was at peace, here he was anxious. He rolled his eyes back, exposing the parts of the eyes that you don't normally see, kind of like an owl, rolling his eyes into the back of his head. He didn't want to look at me like he did at home. I didn't take it as if he was angry at me, I took it as if he was saying I don't want to do this, it's time to go. While I was noticing all this, they gave him a sedative. Not as strong as the one we did at home, as they needed him to stand for the exam, just enough to take the edge off.

The doctor did a physical exam, as well as an ultrasound. He came up with the same findings as earlier. The bladder was very enlarged and there was some kind of blockage or tear in the urethra. He, too, could not find the penis due to the swelling and excess fluids. He agreed with the prior diagnosis and options for treatment. The doctor confirmed surgery would be necessary and that the risk of infection or need to have future surgery again was very high. Llamas have very tiny urinary tracts and it is very difficult to have a successful repair. Based on his history, the vet agreed the likelihood of reoccurrence was high. My decision was for euthanasia. He said they would do it tonight, and that they would do an autopsy, he would telephone me with the results. He believed the autopsy would confirm that we made the right decision.

I didn't ask to stay for the lethal injection. I just gave Perdu a kiss and said goodbye. Ahrynn and I switched out the halter so I could take mine home, empty. As we got in the truck, we could see the doctor going to the cabinet, figuring he was getting the drugs to do the job. We saw Perdu just standing in the squeeze chute, ready and accepting. I told Ahrynn I felt bad because I am always at home with the animals when they die. I am there to sit with them, to comfort them, to give them the most comfortable last few hours I can. I felt as though I just left him in a cold, sterile place with no family, left to die. I knew that before we even got home, he would be gone.

With his suffering over, his new life free of pain, he would move on to a higher place. I also told Ahrynn how lucky we were to believe that this isn't the end for the animals. Their soul merely leaves the physical body and returns to its origin, met by other souls who have passed on earlier. It is so wonderful to know it isn't final for them, merely a change of scenery. My tears weren't for his loss, as I enjoy knowing my animals have passed through the difficulty of pain and sickness to be much better. The tears were for my not being able to be there with him. I am sure if I asked, they would have let me. I didn't even ask, because the look I saw in Perdu's eyes was that he wanted to go alone, he didn't want me to stay. Later, I realized he had said his goodbyes in the field over the last three days. He was just pure love, and that's what he wanted me to remember.

In the morning when I got up, I went to put the trailer away and park the truck in its spot. I took time to reflect back on the day's events and my feelings. A spirit guide spoke and this is what she said:

"You need to write about Perdu. You need to include him in the book you are writing. He, too, has something to say. He already knew he wasn't going to stay and he knew you didn't know that. He understood your intentions and willingness to make him better and he allowed you that opportunity so you would know for certain that you did all you could. He was willing to endure the final pain, the extra trip to the clinic, the extra exams, shots, and all that went with it because he knew you needed to do that. He thanked all of you for giving him such a loving home, a wonderful place to live and feel alive. He knows how much you loved him and the last few days of your time together were special. He needed love and compassion and that's what you gave him. You were pure in your love, with no reservation."

Usually one of our animals who passed on earlier is there to greet another one passing. But for some reason I couldn't think of one that would be there for Perdu. We only had Perdu for a short time and none of the other llamas here had passed yet. I asked the spirit guide, "Who was there to greet Perdu when he arrived?" She said, *"He was surrounded by a large crowd of people, they were cheering him on and touching his neck. He was running through the crowd with his head held high and full of life."*

Then she continued, *"Animals are full of unconditional love. When they pass over, they are in a very high place where it is beautiful, very calm, serene and all the colors are very bright, stronger, sharper, more beautiful than what we see here on earth. Animals know when they have completed their task, did what they came to do. No guilt, no ifs, no wishes (nor 'if I had done' or 'should have done'), it was all done right. They are innocent when they pass, just as they are innocent here, full of love, wanting to be with us and teach us. They know this is their task."*

My mind was blank as I thought what I would write about Perdu. Most of the animals I write about I have had a longer association with. We got Perdu, spent time in initial surgeries and then he was out to pasture. He wasn't the type of llama you could just walk up to. He was always curious, would come to see you, but would only get so far and then stop. If you gestured out to pet him, he would move away. I didn't take him on walks. The only time I really had with him were his recent days of illness. Then I asked the spirit guide one final question, "What shall I write about Perdu?"

As I posed this question, I quieted my mind and emotions, and then I heard: *"Perdu was here to show families that, although you may seem distant in your relationship to each other, even though you may not spend time with each other, you just know that your family exists. When illness or adversity ensues, leave all the chatter behind, come together in PURE LOVE, with unresentful acceptance. Leave the should-of, could-ofs behind, think not of yourself but of the individual who is ill or struggling; offer pure love and compassion."*

Then the guide told me that my animal stories are here to teach people to treat animals as if they have a place in our lives. They are not just four-legged creatures to be left behind, left caged up, beaten and abused, told they are worthless and stupid. These stories are to teach people that animals are PURE LOVE, reflections of ourselves. They take on our pain, sorrow, illness in an attempt to help us, to comfort us. They mirror us. I was told this is another lesson for me, to have had to leave Perdu like I did, to not feel guilty as he had already said his goodbyes earlier. I saw the love in his eyes and didn't realize what he knew.

It's 1:30 in the morning as we drive into the yard with an empty trailer, empty halter and lead rope. Perdu had been euthanized.

*Honor the ability to hear
and use the voice deep within your soul,
for we are the keepers,
the teachers, the students and communicators
of the universe.*
    by Ahrynn McCann

CHAPTER 4

OPAL – A STORY OF ACCEPTANCE

A couple years after we purchased our home, one of our new arrivals was, again, a very sick goat from the auction. Her coat was coarse and spotty, her hips were sunken, her cheeks were drawn and her eyes were sunk in. After taking one look at her, we decided she was very old and we could give her a good home for what time she had left. We couldn't decide on a name, so we just referred to her as "old goat."

One day when I was talking about her to my husband and I said "old goat," he replied, "Olga? Who is Olga?"

I said, "No, Old Goat." Well, that kind of stuck, so she finally had a name – Olga.

Olga grew strong, her spotty coat filled in, she gained weight and her face and eyes filled out. We then realized this "old goat" wasn't old after all. What a complete transformation! All she needed was proper care and love. For many years, she seemed to act as an overseer for the herd, the head goat. Despite her initial illness, she gave birth to many healthy babies.

My husband and I were out in the prairie doing chores when we noticed Olga had that all-too-familiar "bubble" hanging from under her tail, an indication her baby's delivery would be within an hour or so. We were surprised, as Olga had not shown any signs of nearing delivery. Her belly hadn't dropped, and she didn't have the large, engorged mammary milk sack. She didn't appear to be having any contractions. Even though we weren't expecting Olga to deliver this early, we knew she never had problems and always had just one, very big baby.

Our ranch chores took a couple hours. All the while we kept an eye on Olga. Afternoon turned to evening, and she still hadn't delivered and didn't show any signs of progression, but she didn't show signs of a struggle, either. Becoming concerned, I decided to stay at the barn and observe Olga just in case she needed assistance.

By 10 p.m. Olga was having slight contractions, but nothing to start getting excited about. At 10:30, Michael came down to the barn to check on us. I told him she wasn't much better; however, the contractions seemed a little closer. She had a couple hard pushes but no further progress in the delivery stage. I told him I did some Reiki on her, which seemed to help. It just seemed as though she was struggling and needed some assistance. The Reiki calmed her.

Given the circumstances, Michael decided to stay with us. By 11:30 we were well into hard labor and actually saw a foot start to appear. But only one foot. Olga pushed again, but still only one foot. At first glance it appeared as though it was a back foot. Concerned about a breech delivery, Michael looked closer and confirmed it was a front foot. With relief, we believed our earlier thoughts of complications were unwarranted. We decided to stay for the delivery, just in case.

Another push, a hard one at that, along with a painful cry, but we still only had one foot. Michael decided Olga was going to need help. With some hot, soapy water, alcohol and hydrogen peroxide, he sterilized his hands and began to assist Olga. With his hands and forearms inside Olga's birth canal, he could only find the one front foot. Michael asked me to watch Olga, as she might become more uncomfortable as he felt around inside for the other foot. After a few minutes, he believed he found it – bent backwards, knee facing forward. With some effort, Michael was able to extend the foot into the birth canal. Pulling on two feet as Olga continued to push, we had two very long legs, then more legs, but no head. A normal birth presentation is with the head between the two front legs.

While Olga rested for a minute, we noticed the mucous covering on the legs was a greenish-yellow color, which didn't look healthy. The legs were very lifeless. Our previous worries of an abortion resurfaced – we figured we had a dead baby to deliver. Certainly with the length of time it took to find the second leg, the color of the membrane and the lifeless legs, there wasn't any way this baby could be alive.

We had a cell phone at the barn so I called the veterinarian. At that time of night, I was only able to leave a voice message. There wasn't an emergency number provided, and we considered this an emergency. We were Olga's only help.

We couldn't just sit and do nothing while we waited for a return call from the vet. Considering the two possible positions the head could be in –

downward in the pelvic area or sideways at the neck – Michael reached into the birth canal one more time to find the baby's head. Still unable to find it, we did the only thing we could do, keep pulling on the legs.

As he pulled, Olga pushed, each big contraction in unison with the pulling. After three or four big pushes and pulls, we felt the baby move through the canal without getting hung up. Olga was in extreme pain. I was holding her head, continuing with Reiki to ease her labor, help her dilate and comfort her while Michael was pulling. To our surprise, we saw a bulge. It appeared to be the butt end. We both looked at each other and, once again, thought breech delivery, but he had two front feet. Without warning, Olga gave another big push and a loud cry, and out came the neck with the head to follow. The neck had been turned to the side with the head up against the shoulder.

We were in awe of the delivery, then we noticed the baby was actually alive. After we quickly removed the greenish membrane from its mouth, the baby appeared to be taking its last breath. Not willing to give up so easily, Michael began CPR and mouth-to-mouth resuscitation. He was elated to find a strong heartbeat and another breath. We moved the baby toward Olga's head so she could do what mother goats do, lick the baby to stimulate heart and lungs. By some miracle the baby continued to breathe.

As Olga cleaned off her new baby girl, we noticed there was a large amount of sticky, tar-like fecal matter at the baby's rear end. We became concerned about infection. Did the baby ingest the bad membrane? Did the fecal matter cause the membrane to become infected? Had the baby been overdue and stressed, which caused the baby to expel fecal matter? We didn't hold much hope for this baby's survival. In addition to the delivery issues, we were concerned about Olga. Invading the birth canal can cause infection for her, too.

After Olga cleaned the baby, we began to examine it. Not good. Her left front leg was crooked, her knee and ankle turned out to the left. (This was the leg Michael had to find and unbend to make the delivery.) It almost seemed arthritic. The knee and ankle joints were very hard, wouldn't straighten. One shoulder was dropped and dislodged. It had "free movement" to it. It reminded us of someone who is double-jointed. That shoulder was lower than the other shoulder and lay flat. We could move it without any reaction of pain, but the shoulder wouldn't stay. In feeling it, it seemed to have fluid movement. The other shoulder seemed to be in proper alignment. The ribs, backbone and buttocks were twisted. Her tail was off-center. She couldn't put any weight on either front leg. The right front leg was normal, but she was lopsided without the other front leg fully extending.

In addition to leg and shoulder issues, she couldn't hold her head up. Her head was much too heavy, and she didn't have neck strength. She could not stand up. Her back legs were strong and she knew they worked, but with the front legs not working and a heavy head, she could not get herself up.

Olga, on the other hand, being the excellent mom she was, knew it was imperative that the baby get up to nurse. Becoming impatient, frustrated and somewhat aggressive, Olga kept pawing at her baby to get up.

Concerned Olga might unintentionally strike the baby, we decided one of us would need to stay at the barn. I volunteered. We put two plastic bags of shaved bedding end to end, which provided a raised cot for me to sleep on. Michael then hung two heat lamps above me, one above my head, the other above my legs. We got a sleeping bag and I was set. He hung two towels and a plastic feed bag over the window openings of the barn to keep the cold out. Just like camping!

My job was to observe. To make sure Olga didn't step on, sleep on or otherwise cause harm to the baby. I also needed to be sure she nursed. We gave Olga penicillin for possible infection and a douche to help combat any infection, as well. We gave the baby selenium and penicillin, and a bed of straw to support her head.

Whoever said a barn is quiet at night was wrong. I didn't really expect to sleep, but I sure wanted to get as many five-minute "power naps" as possible. I could hear a few mice scouring around in the grain bucket looking for a midnight snack. The goat in the next stall was eating all night. The metal feeder was on the common wall, so each grabbing of the feed was heard. Then the chewing and water drinking. Two stalls down, another mother was snoring. Three stalls down, the triplets were awake, playing, bouncing off the walls. The llamas were pacing back and forth on the concrete sidewalk in front of the barn. Birds were flying here and there all night. I could even hear planes drop their wheels in anticipation of landing in Sacramento. Then, of course, every time Olga or the baby cried, I jumped up to observe. Was Olga stepping on her? Laying on her? Pawing her? Or was she just calling to her? A barn is not a quiet place at night!

Olga and I talked. She looked me square in the eye as if to say, "Why are you here? You have never slept in the barn before; why now? This is my time with my baby and I can do just fine!" I explained to her that her baby had some physical challenges and, although she is an excellent mom, her baby could not get up to walk or nurse and needed our help in order to survive. She seemed okay with that, and I believe she and I finally got some sleep. Not much, but some.

I tried twice during the night to get the baby to nurse from Olga. She wouldn't. Although she couldn't stand, she was such a large baby she could lay on her belly and still reach Olga's teat. Problem being, she couldn't hold her head up. I tried to support her head. As with all babies, she didn't like the restraint and fought terribly to get away. Considering all she had been through, I took the path of least resistance and pumped milk from Olga to bottle-feed the baby.

From time to time we have to assist a mother with delivery but then the mother usually takes over from there. Not this time. It was like having a newborn of our own. Unable to walk or hold its head up, we knew there would be nothing typical about this one. Olga is an excellent mom, but she was going to need a full-time nanny – ME.

Michael and I had wanted to name her "darn lucky" or "miracle." We knew it wouldn't be permanent and thought we might wait a few days to see if she survived. Our daughter, Ahrynn, took one look at her and said her name is OPAL because her eyes looked like opals. So, Opal it was.

The first few days were spent administering medications and assessing Opal's physical limitations and abilities. It was a rigorous schedule. I knew she still couldn't nurse, so I pumped Olga again and bottle-fed Opal. I started to do therapy, holding her head strong so she could eventually hold it up on her own. Since she was able to put weight on her back legs, I supported her chest and head to counterbalance. Opal never seemed to tire or complain.

After spending an hour working with Opal, I realized we needed an apparatus that would allow her to stand, support her belly, let her touch the ground and try to stand on her feet without falling over, something that would support her head. I shared this idea with Michael. In between feeding the rest of the farm animals and organizing the workers for the day, Michael built the apparatus. He came to the barn to show me his masterpiece; "Is this what you were thinking of?" he said. It was perfect!

Michael had made a short saw horse covered with carpet padding and secured a plastic cup to the top for head support. Opal could put pressure on her back legs to practice standing and strengthen her neck with cup support. At this level, she could see things differently. In the stall, all she could do was lay on her belly with her chin flat on the ground. This device would allow her to work at her own pace.

The apparatus quickly became known as "the therapy board." The plan was to get the back legs strong, get her holding her head up and then work on getting her to use her front legs. She could use her left front leg if she knelt, but I was still not sure of the actual shoulder movement or support for that leg yet. One thing at a time.

I kept a daily journal to track this adventure, as I already knew there were going to be a lot of details. The journal included entries for morning, afternoon and evening, sometimes just details of medications, therapy sessions and, of course, progress and surprises. Although every day was special to us, the full journal would be much too detailed for this story. The original version was over 100 full-size pages. The most difficult part of writing is the condensing, and this story was intended to be a chapter, not an entire book. Therefore, I have included only highlights from the journal days, and some days have been omitted completely.

DAY ONE
Olga and Opal received penicillin. Therapy on the block for four sessions (1-2 hours each time). Olga is very patient. She isn't stir crazy yet from being in the stall this long with a baby that can't get up. Last feeding 10:30 p.m. Mom and Opal slept in the stall and I slept in the house.

DAY TWO
I was worried because Opal hadn't eaten since 10:30 the night before, so I rushed down to the barn. Olga wouldn't let me pump milk, but Charlie Brown, another goat, let me have some of hers. I held the bottle up high and did not support Opal's head while she

drank. It took quite a while to empty the bottle, as she could not hold her head up long before it fell. I took the therapy board outside, figuring Opal would enjoy seeing all the other babies playing. They were curious about her and came over to sniff. She loved watching everything. Before she could only hear the other babies from her stall, now she could see them. The time on the board went much faster when she was entertained. I took Opal off the board and tried some freestanding. In the afternoon I brought her outside again and we did the same routine. Then I carried her around in my arms while tending to other farm duties. Opal was already holding her head up on her own. Holding her under the chest with her back legs dangling free put her head in a different position and made it easier for her to hold it up and look around. I held her up on the fence so she could rest her chin on the rail. She moved her head from side to side to watch the other goats. For the late-afternoon feeding, she was able to hold her head up longer. We were progressing very quickly. At 10 p.m. I went down for the last feeding and did some therapy on the board. She was using her front legs more to push up. Olga was being difficult about giving milk, but she gave in. Opal drank from the bottle without me helping to hold her head up. She was able to stand on her own for a short few moments. She rests on the knee of the left front leg and stretches the right front leg straight out in front of her and manages to balance that way. She can't stand long on her own, but her will is extremely strong.

DAY THREE

Opal heard me come through the gate to the barn and started to cry because she knew I would bring milk. Olga would not give milk, so Charlie Brown obliged again. I put the therapy block outside the stall. It is as if I can read her thoughts. Opal sees the others walking and jumping and is trying to figure out how to do the same. I let her try some more freestanding. I kept trying to get her to bend her front leg, but she seems to have figured out her own way to stand. She still needs some help to support her chest and head. We usually feed the moms up on the hill in front of the barn, but Olga is reluctant to go. We have to lead her up there. She is an excellent mother with lots of patience. In the afternoon, I took Olga and Opal to the middle prairie with the other moms and babies. I set the therapy board on a platform right in the middle of the others and Opal seemed content just to watch. She didn't push and try to get off like she had before. The days had been foggy, but today the sun came out. Olga wouldn't go out and graze; she stayed right next to the platform, but she didn't push away other babies that came near. I placed Opal on the grass and she was able to get into her stance very quickly and stayed for a longer time. She would fall slowly to the ground and get herself back up. I left her on the grass in the sun while I did other chores. When I came back about an hour later, Olga was still standing next to her baby. What dedication this mother has! In the evening, Opal cried when she heard me come through the gate. I used formula instead of waking Charlie Brown.

Opal held her head up on her own for the entire feeding. She was even "hitting" it like the other babies do to get more milk faster. We spent a little time on the block. She spent most of the time freestanding. Opal is able to lift her head up and down as well as side to side. She was actually trying to move her feet, moving in a backward direction rather than forward.

DAY FOUR
Opal sat on her therapy board and watched the others play and seems more alert. Several of the other babies jump up and sniff her nose and snoodle with her. When she tries to walk she tends to go backwards.

DAY FIVE

Opal went with us to do farm chores, and I held her in my arms. She loves this position because she can see so much. I must have packed her around for over an hour. We did therapy on and off the board. At one point, she fell sound asleep on the board with her head supported on the cup. She looked content. I arrived home from work late and Michael was already feeding. When he opened the barn door I could see Opal standing all by herself. I sat with her and held her in my arms and told her I missed spending time with her. I massaged her and she fell asleep in my arms. When I put her down, she got into her standing position and was able to relax to the ground and get back up three times in a row. She is so willing and smart! Just yesterday I still had to hold her head while she was standing, and tonight I didn't hold her head up once.

On the fifth day of Opal's life, Ahrynn called me at work and asked if Opal had talked to me yet. I told her no, but I felt very strongly she was present to provide an example. Ahrynn said Opal had spoken to her and asked if I had time to listen to what she said. I was delighted to listen. Here is Ahrynn's account of her communication with Opal.

"*I was writing in my journal for High School English class. Every day we get about 30 minutes just to write in our journals, and I use this time to center myself and clear my busy thoughts. Today my quote or thought was: 'Too often we look with our mind and not with our heart.' Almost seconds after I wrote that, Opal said she wanted to tell me things that would not only change our outlook for her but also of life.*

"*She is* Forgiving. *She sees the* Importance in life, *not the disadvantages. She knows she is different not mentally or spiritually but physically. Then she asked me: Why do others judge? This was the main point Opal wants us to* figure out or find within ourselves. The next part of her message sent chills up my spine and adrenaline through my veins. She is the Speaker Of The Souls. She has great Knowledge Of Acceptance. She grows spiritually every day. The Universe has sent her to us to show how we judge by physical appearance too much. Once she has taught us this and we understand (not just say we understand but have faith and trust with ourselves and with Opal), she will walk. We must put Faith beyond reasoning.

"She said her physical difference is the only thing holding her behind, but being the beautiful soul she is, she is grateful to have the support of everyone and the love. She knows she is here to teach and she is happy she is being taught at the same time.

"She then got very excited and said, 'Oh by the way, Opal is a perfect name for me because it is a Precious Stone of the Underworld (afterlife),' and that is what she wants us to focus on because she teaches from her Underworld (afterlife), which is Her Soul. I thanked her over and over again for the teachings she has brought to us. We are very blessed to have Opal in our lives, and she thanked us in return for our confidence in her and the Grace we bring to and for each other in a continuing circle that evolves around our Souls."

The next day, Ahrynn called me and said Opal had talked to her again. "She (Opal) wants to run and play with the other babies, so she found within herself how to subconsciously put herself out with them, almost like an out-of-body experience. She did this so she would have muscle memory and be able to work her legs. The disadvantage of an out-of-body experience is you can't always bring back what you experienced. So Opal, while running and playing with the other babies, is not able to bring all the muscle movement back with her, but she could stand better after her experience."

When I went down for the evening feeding on Day Six, Opal heard the gate and cried. I picked her up and Olga got in the way, always wanting to be sure she is beside her baby. Other mothers who are not nursing would give up on the baby and abandon it, but not Olga. Olga is teaching us that we must stay by each other's side, even if they can't do the things we can or are less fortunate. We must not cast them aside; we must give them support.

After therapy time, I picked up Opal, held her and thanked her for her determination, for speaking to Ahrynn and communicating her message to us, for being here and offering to teach us. I thanked Olga for bringing her baby to our place and being willing to bear the burden of the restrictions this type of dedication requires, the sacrifice she is making. After a short rest, Opal went back to work and this time she walked backwards. On bended knee, she pulled her shoulder back toward her back legs by dragging it on the ground, then she put her nose to the ground, twisted her head and pushed herself backward while pulling her front right leg back at the same time.

Then she moved both back legs backward at the same time. It was quite a process to watch. When this was done, she did it two more times in a row without missing a beat! Why backwards and not forwards, I am not sure, but she is walking. I picked her up and praised her. I told her how proud I was that she figured this out. I put her back down to sleep. She knows she did something different, and I can just imagine what she will be dreaming. It is amazing how much she has changed her world in six short days. I can hardly wait to see what the next few days will bring.

DAY SEVEN

Opal seems to have perfected her backwards walking and now picks up her left front leg on bended knee and moves it backwards and then sets it back on the ground while balancing on the other three legs. You can see her thinking about the process. It was very encouraging and enlightening to watch this. What is her drive? What is her interest? What makes her strive to do more? Would another goat have just given up? She isn't satisfied with just dragging her leg to walk, she wants to lift it up! We walked the width of the stall, not once but twice! She put in quite a workout, drank some milk and went to bed.

DAY EIGHT

This evening I got the impression Opal wanted to practice balance, not walking. She didn't attempt to walk, just stood and stretched her head from side to side, reaching her nose to her belly. She didn't teeter, sway or fall. She nibbled at hay stems and other things near her. She was very present in her surroundings. I held her in my arms for a rest. Olga came over to snoodle her nose to nose, and Opal rubbed her cheek on Olga's face. It is so wonderful to see them connecting this way.

DAY NINE

Tonight Opal doesn't need minute-to-minute support. She has strengthened herself physically and mentally, and I am there just to keep her company. She stands for long periods of time, moves her legs and, when she falls or begins to fall, still manages to get back up. She is so independent, but she can't take off running yet.

On Day Ten Ahrynn and I went out to the movies and then to a book store. Ahrynn was looking for a special book, and I was just browsing when I heard the suggestion to look for something on judgment. Ahrynn and I went to the computer and typed in "judgment." We didn't like the results, just didn't feel right. We went to a few sections in the store, but neither of us felt compelled to pick something up. Then I went down the aisle for "appearance" (all the stuff on beauty, acne, decreasing facial lines, etc.) and found a book called *Conscious Healing* by John Selby. It was about healing yourself from the inside and strengthening your immune system.

I wondered why I would pick up that book, then randomly turned to page 84. This is what it said: "When we accept something, we open ourselves to being influenced by it. We allow this something to exist with us in our world, we grant it space to live. We need make no effort to deal with things around us that we accept because we are in harmony with them and can accept their influence on us. Acceptance means participation with something or someone; it means interaction." (*Conscious Healing*, page 84)

I read it to Ahrynn and she said, "This has something to do with Opal. Remember when Opal spoke to me she talked of acceptance. She said she is here to help us understand acceptance without judging. It is not a coincidence that you found this book in a section entitled 'appearance' and the random page you flipped to and the only paragraph you read dealt with acceptance. The Universe is at work; we just need to listen and respond."

And The Animals Will Teach Us is once again proven so true. Just imagine, we walked through the doors of the bookstore, a large bookstore, and standing among the thousands of books, we went to a certain section, and amid all the shelves, amid all the books on the shelves, selected that one book and randomly flipped to a page and read one paragraph. How else could this happen other than Universal guidance and energy? Opal had guided us to where she wanted us to go. We had already been to another bookstore looking for the book Ahrynn wanted, but they were out, so we went to this bookstore. This bookstore had the book Ahrynn wanted in a display of best sellers right as we walked in, thereby freeing our minds to be receptive to Opal's message.

The thought popped into my mind to find something on judgment, but it wasn't judgment, it was "acceptance." If we *accept*, we aren't judging. When we learn to accept it means we aren't judging. Opal said to Ahrynn she has great *knowledge of acceptance*. It is not a coincidence that this soul who has knowledge of acceptance directed us to that paragraph in that book on that shelf in that section of a great big bookstore!

In the evening I spent time with Opal *just being*. I just wanted to absorb what she was doing. I looked at her, so innocent and patient, trying to get all her limbs to work in unison, and thanked her for what she taught us today. I thanked her for the sacrifice she was making and again thanked Olga for her sacrifice as well. As I watched, I realized she could use a new therapy board, one with a thin, flat platform and a nonslip cover to give her more support when she is standing. I am anxious to have the new board ready for her. We had not used her original therapy board in many days – another milestone for her.

DAY ELEVEN

This morning I took Opal out to the straw bales we had stacked in the barn area for the babies to play on. She liked being up so high to look around. Olga liked it, too; they stood cheek-to-cheek and Opal nibbled on Olga's ear. Once Opal was knocked down when one of the babies jumped from one straw bale to another. She didn't seem to mind, just tried to stand back up with no whining or fussing. Other babies rubbed against her or fell into her, but she stayed standing. One of the babies even chewed on Opal's ear and she turned and smelled its nose. The others didn't seem to treat her any different; they don't know she can't walk and they have to be careful around her. They just play as usual, no holding back.

This day was different than the others. Opal was exhibiting energy that could be seen inward and outward. Her head was held high when I walked into the stall to feed her. She had a glisten in her eyes. When I picked her up to feed her, she was squirming and wanted down, ready to go. I had to let her drink the bottle while standing. As she was standing, she was full of energy, her head was constantly moving up, down and sideways. She had a glow about her. She was "talking" a lot and actually trying to eat some hay. She was only one and a half weeks old. At this age, all the babies start to explore what their mothers are eating, and I was glad to see Opal's curiosity. It was like she wanted to show me what she had learned and was putting all the steps together more quickly and making her moves faster, even trying to go forward. Whenever I picked her up, she was like a child who wants down to run and play. I was absolutely amazed. I rubbed her all over and put her down and away she went, backward. As I watched her energy, I got the impression she had spent the last six hours practicing in her head so she could show me what she could do. Then I remembered what Opal had told Ahrynn about how she subconsciously practiced running and playing with the others.

DAY TWELVE

I was finally able to take my new therapy board down to the barn. Opal loved it. She immediately skated across it in three quick but very precisely calculated moves backward. She is so full of life. She is curious about herself, others and her surroundings. For the first time, I saw her startled by a movement, and she seemed to want to smell the roses for the first time. She is now standing on all three legs with her left front leg just dangling in the air. When Olga nudged her, she stumbled a little but quickly regained her balance. For the first time, I saw her resting on both front knees. We did a little therapy where I helped her go from kneeling to standing, and Opal caught on very quickly. Opal has quite a personality. She doesn't need us as much anymore. At two weeks old, she is growing up.

DAY FOURTEEN

OPAL WALKED FORWARD! It was only two steps, but it was forward! As I was heating the bottle for her, I heard her crying in the stall next door. I tried to pick her up to stand so she could drink and she wouldn't have it; she wanted to stand herself without my help.

And she did. She wiggled her back legs underneath her and up she went! I gave her the bottle, in awe of what she had done. I told her she must think all day about what and how she is going to surprise us next. She has made such progress it is hard to believe she is only two weeks old. When she took a break from the bottle, I held it out a little in front of her and that's when she walked forward to get it. Another major surprise! This morning she couldn't stand up by herself or walk forward; tonight, she had it all figured out. What a champ!

DAY SIXTEEN

We put Opal and Olga in the middle prairie with Patches and the triplets she had borne just the day before. They would be good company, as they wouldn't push her over and would stick close to their mom. Opal seemed to like the green grass and was nibbling at it. In the evening, she followed me around the stall, turning in circles to go the other direction. She walked forward very quickly without hesitation, not pausing to think which leg to move. It was becoming natural for her. If this is all she does, she will be able to live a full life, hobbling on three legs. She may eventually run the length of the field like a three-legged dog and not miss a beat. She doesn't know anything different, she just accepts her condition for what it is. Two weeks ago, she couldn't walk or hold her head up. Determination, a strong will, acceptance and dreaming brought her where she is.

DAY SEVENTEEN

Opal has become very independent. She gets herself up and doesn't like being held. She doesn't use her head to assist in walking anymore. I feel like my child has grown up, learned to drive and is living on her own!

As I look back on the days since her birth, I realize Opal made major progress because she focused each day on just that day. What can I do today? What can I manage? What can I learn? What can I practice? By focusing on just one thing, she was now walking! She figured out a pattern that worked and wasn't worried about whether or not she was going in the right direction or doing it right. She just knew she was moving. As Ahrynn said in her communication with Opal, she would "dream walk," practicing it outside her body, then come back and put it into action. She didn't lay around and sulk or wish; she planned then acted. This is truly an example of living in the present moment. By being so present, Opal was able to stay focused and direct her energy to one task. Focusing her energy got results – she could now walk forward and in circles.

In the afternoon I went down to feed Opal a snack. I had put her in the barn stall but left the gate open so everyone else could go in and out. I was surprised to see Olga in the field with the other mammas and babies. Olga never left Opal, so I went to the barn to check on her. Opal was all by herself on the old hay in front of the barn. That meant she had walked from the back of her stall to the front (about 20 feet), across the sidewalk (4 feet) and out onto the old hay. She was just hanging out like it was no big thing. I couldn't believe she had actually walked that far. I don't know how long it took her, but the idea she decided to go for a walk on her own was wonderful.

That evening when I picked her up, Opal was quiet and seemed to like being held close. I thanked her for the lessons she had taught us, the message of acceptance, by showing us every day she accepted herself and, by doing this, she was able to excel beyond expectations. She told us she would walk when we understood, and she is walking. I don't know if she will ever have full extended use of her left front leg. If not, she will manage just fine. Maybe she will choose not to ever fully use that leg so every time we see her out in the pasture, we will remember. When a visitor asks us what happened to that poor goat, we can tell them the story and tell them of acceptance, not judgment. They should not feel sorry for her, it is not how someone looks or appears, it is what is inside their soul, their heart. Opal is a wonderful soul, she is strong, determined, focused and accomplishes what she sets out to do. We can learn from her; she was sent here to teach us.

On February 6, I went down to the barn for the usual feeding and then took Opal up to the pasture to be with the others. I sat her down on the ground and started to walk away to get feed for the others, but she was there beside me. Opal had followed and kept pace with me.

I was so surprised, I picked her up and put her back up in the field a ways so I could watch her as I walked away. What a character! She was actually "skipping" on her three legs, holding her front left leg up and balancing well enough to hop and skip on the other three. I picked her up and held her for a few minutes, rubbing my face against hers, giving her kisses and love while rubbing her with my hand. When I set her down, she followed me again. I decided today was an Opal day, so she went with me.

By February 14, Opal was sleeping with "the gang." When I went down for the morning and evening feedings, she was not listening for me to come through the gate. When I call her name, she cries to let me know where she is and comes running for her milk. She plows through the others. She is so cute. Her light caramel color and brown eyes make you want to cuddle her.

A few days earlier when I was feeding, all the goats came running, but Opal was in the way. I was curious how she was going to manage to not get trampled. She started to run with them but realized she wasn't quite fast enough, so she moved to the side of the pack and waited for them to pass, then she ran after the herd by herself. When the other babies push her around, she stands her ground. She doesn't fall; she just moves out of the way and turns to look at them as if to say, "That wasn't very nice at all." It will be interesting to see if she starts to push back.

Opal runs to us when we call her name. She can run quickly on three legs, then she drops her left front leg for a few steps, then runs on three legs again. She has another technique where she slides the left front leg while bending the right front at the knee and pushing with the back legs. This reduces shoulder movement and appears to be less effort, but she doesn't get as far as fast.

Today a family came to our ranch, interested in purchasing goats to clear star thistle on their ten acres. As we stood at the fence, Opal heard me talking to them and came running over. They said how sad it was she was like that and asked if she would always be that way. I told them she had been that way since birth, but she doesn't want us to feel sorry for her, just accept her. They said, "Well, she probably doesn't know any difference."

I told them, "She doesn't miss a thing and she thinks she is just like the rest of the goats." I was glad to have the opportunity to tell others Opal's message of acceptance.

When I took Two-Bitts, the black Lab, to the vet, I inquired about getting x-rays for Opal to see if her bones were fused, her rib cage tilted, etc. When the vet called, I explained what we had gone through with Opal and how I had kept a journal of her progress. He said he would discuss it with the other doctors and let me know if they would donate the x-rays, as the cost would be prohibitive. A few days later, the doctor called and we set a time for Opal to see him.

This vet usually deals with small animals like dogs, cats and birds, so seeing Opal was a treat for him. As usual, she was charming and didn't fuss or try to get away. She is so accepting and submits to whatever we need to do to take care of her. It is as if she knows we are helping her and all this fussing is a result of her willingness to come and teach us about acceptance. She knows this is part of that choice, and she is playing her part exceptionally well.

I had brought my journal with me to show the doctor. I showed him the pictures of her birth, the therapy boards and her social play. He was impressed with the dedication these showed.

The x-rays showed Opal's bones were not fused and both legs appeared to be the same length and growing just fine. It appeared the tendons were too short and were pulling the left leg backward. He thought surgery would be effective and had an opening the next day, so we scheduled Opal for surgery.

Opal had her surgery on March 3, 2004. She couldn't have her bottle before surgery, just a small amount of water. I told her she could ride on the floor of the car in the front if she didn't make a sound or a mess. She didn't fuss the whole time. She is such a good traveler! You almost want to take her everywhere you go, just like a dog.

When the vet called to say Opal was ready to be picked up, Michael took a bottle because he knew she would be hungry. He commented on how good she travels. She snuggled down on the floor and was just present.

Opal had a straight leg! We were told to keep the splint on for one week and then go in for a recheck. Our cost for the surgery was about $300, and we were happy to pay it. When we called to set an appointment for a recheck, they only wanted the doctor who did the surgery to see her, but he was not available for almost two weeks. That meant Opal would be in the splint for longer.

When I took her to see the doctor, he said how wonderful she was to have around, how easy-going she was. He told me Opal's rib cage was tilted and compromised, but she was just fine. He unwrapped her splint and said her leg looked really good. We would need to exercise her leg by bending it at the knee to keep things moving. I told him we would do whatever was necessary to ensure the best possible recovery.

Things got busy at the office and at home, and I wasn't writing in the journal like I normally would. Opal seemed to be regressing. I had been exercising her leg and she was so good to work with, but she had been running a fever. I scheduled another visit with the vet and put a homemade splint on her leg. It was swollen and hot and appeared to be very uncomfortable. It also appeared her leg was beginning to bend back again. When the vet saw her, her temperature was 105.9 (normal is 101). He put her on antibiotics. I told him she wasn't putting any weight on her leg and was back to dragging it. The therapy was difficult because the leg was so swollen and hot. Opal was tolerant and never complained, but when we tried to bend the leg, she would raise her nose and whimper a bit.

The antibiotics worked and Opal's fever was gone. She was putting weight on her leg and all seemed normal. Opal was all grown up now and didn't want to be fussed with. Sometimes when I picked her up to hold her, she acted as though it hurt, like everything inside was crushed and uncomfortable. I tried to just pet and scratch her (she loves to have the top of her butt scratched). She gets her head and shoulders turned around to watch me scratch her, and then she falls over because she is off-balance. I don't have as much daily interaction with Opal, as she goes out and grazes and plays with the other goats. She eats well. Since Opal was self-sufficient, the journal entries stopped.

On Saturday night, October 27, Ahrynn was sleeping in her room and I was in the family room working on projects. Ahrynn came in and said, "Mom, you have to come to my room, but you must be very quiet. I hear things in the ceiling like footsteps, and my door keeps moving and making creaky sounds, but the door is closed."

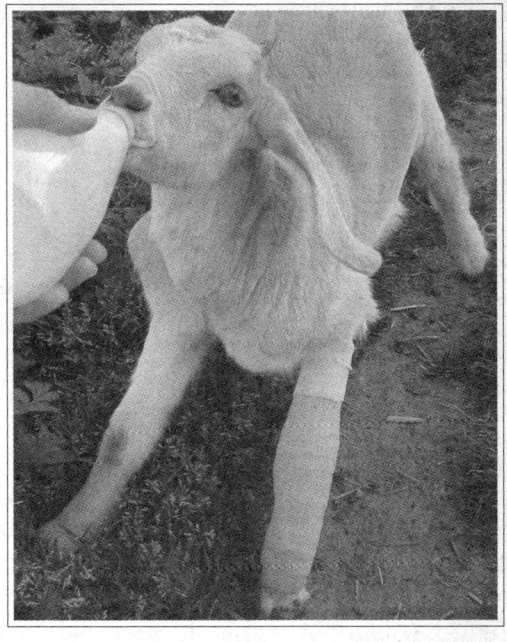

We went through her brother's room so we would not have to open her bedroom door. When we got into her room, she climbed into bed and I stood still to listen. I didn't hear anything, She begged me to wait longer, but still nothing. So I left. A few minutes later, she came out and got me again. She said the noises returned the moment I left.

This time I climbed into bed with her and we listened once more. I did not hear any sounds in the ceiling, but I did hear the door creak. It banged in its own jamb casing like the wind was blowing through an open window, but there was no wind and no open window. Ahrynn said she could "feel things" and sensed it was a spirit of some kind.

She didn't want it to be a bad spirit. I couldn't feel any presence, but she certainly did. We asked that the spirit guides cleanse the room and that only good spirits be present, they were welcome to share our space. I asked if the spirit was evil and I received the answer "No." When I asked if it was a good spirit, the answer again was "No." Then I asked if it was a neutral spirit and received a confirmation. I was surprised, as I had never thought of a "neutral" spirit before and do not even know what caused me to ask such a question.

I told Ahrynn the spirit was neutral, neither bad nor good. She was once again overwhelmed with the feeling of a spirit present. It only happened when she was in the room alone. When I was there, the ceiling noises stopped and the door was still. I told her this entity was reaching out to her and to not be afraid, accept it and all would be revealed in time. I told her to take notice of what was happening and be open to the events. With that, I left the room and went back to my projects.

The next morning I went down to the barn to feed. The hay was up at the third pasture in the hay barn, so I fed the goats in the third prairie first. Then I took hay to the middle pasture, where Opal, Olga, Patches, Rescue and her baby and both of BG's babies were being kept. I noticed Opal wasn't there and knew she never missed a meal. I went looking and found her in the barn where I had fed the day before. She was dead.

I was shocked and surprised. She had not been ill, feverish or off her feed. Just the day before, she was acting her usual self. I placed her body in the wheel barrel and took her over to Olga so I knew Olga had seen her and knew she was dead. Olga sniffed her and turned away to continue eating, as if to say, "I know. I was with her when she died."

I went back to the house and told Michael Opal was dead. He was just as surprised as I was. Not surprised that she had died, but surprised she had died without any warning. From the day Opal was born, we knew it would be harder for her to survive because her insides had been so turned and twisted. Opal didn't miss anything. She ate with the other goats, she played and rustled for food out in the field, and she walked great distances every day. She never gave in to her disability; she saw it as just the way she was and there wasn't anything different. As she grew, we could see she had a harder time. Her breathing was labored and she panted even on cooler days. After eating, her sides would expand to accommodate the food because there just wasn't enough room inside with everything so twisted. We knew the extra weight on her front left shoulder and leg was causing problems. Even though she could walk, it always looked as though her shoulder was dislocated; it wasn't, it was just her way of compensating.

When Ahrynn woke the day after her visit from the spirit, I told her the entity in her room was Opal. I explained, "She died and was coming to you." We didn't understand why Opal would come to Ahrynn, since I spent more time with her doing therapy, massages and color therapy. Yes, Ahrynn was part of Opal's life, too, but it seemed odd. And the fact the entity stopped making its presence known when I came into the room seemed odd, too.

A few days later, I was speaking with Linda, a special friend who is very spiritual and can see things from the other side. She had known Opal, so I told her Opal had died and told her about the night before and what happened with Ahrynn. She immediately said, "I am seeing that Opal came to Ahrynn to let her know she may be called upon to assist in the work along with you regarding the animals. Opal's spirit passing through in such a manner that only Ahrynn could sense her was a message meant only for Ahrynn. That is why you could not sense it."

As we continued our conversation, Linda said, "Did you know all the colors of the chakras are in the opal?" I said I didn't and my body tingled. I immediately thought I would get a ring, a very special ring, I would wear every day to inspire me to think of Opal, to remember what she stood for. I would tell her story to all who asked about my ring. Tears welled up in my eyes, as they are now as I write this. When I got home, I shared Linda's and my conversation with Ahrynn.

I starting thinking about Opal rings. I knew I wanted the stone to be the most important part, the band didn't matter. The stone would reflect the symbol of Opal's life. I didn't want diamonds or other gem stones or a large band, just something simple. I asked Ahrynn if she would pick it out.

On Christmas day that year, I was presented with two rings in one box. Ahrynn said the one she was drawn to appeared to be more to her taste and likes, so she selected another ring that was more what I liked. Along with the rings came a note from Ahrynn. I started to read it but couldn't get past the first sentence without tears. I told her I would have to set it aside and read it later after all the gifts were opened.

Later that afternoon, I sat quietly by myself in front of the fireplace and read the letter.

"The ring symbolizes not only unity between human and animal but an understanding of voices as well. Opal was our guide, our teacher of a world that is so judgmental. Her guidance grew as we learned from each lesson. As she came to share with us the life she agreed too, she took with her a piece of our heart, soul and mind to the other side. We must continue showing many what we did for her, how we helped her grow, to see inside **'The Opal Within Us.'**

"Mom, at the time I did not know why Opal wanted that name. An opal from the depths of the ocean is not perfect, may not have all the unique color one wishes for, but Opal said she was not perfect, either; her soul and heart were well-centered but not perfect. The opal she wishes you to have is one of many, but when you see these opals, do you see her inside of them? The fire inside of the opal represents Opal's determination, always wanting to take the next step no matter the pain. And when you see this fire in the opal stone, Opal is reminding you when you are feeling pain, discomfort or hopelessness, look into this stone and find her within you – she left a piece of herself within you as well, and now she will be with you for eternity.

"Opal spoke to me. She said: *'You helped me feel contentment and understand the human touch and your voice offered reassurance. Your energy was endless. I cannot explain how the color therapy helped me, but it filled me with tingling sensations throughout my body. I knew beforehand I would pass on to the other side, not leaving you but guiding you.'* Opal showed me a hill, a place of peace, a sacred treasure that she found. Opal continued: *'LOVE – between friends, human and animal, to us we are one. We live in a kingdom where hope, grace, unity and love surround us each day. I passed on these elements of forgiveness, faith, guidance, trust and the uniqueness that one's heart and soul makes the physical body healthy. My time was short but well-lived. And yes, with my physical difference, I LIVED! I LIVED! I am still living within you. You gave me the ability and strength to live, to teach, to share with you as a healer we, in turn, heal ourselves. It is now my turn to heal you'.*"

I read the letter three times. Ahrynn said she wrote it Christmas Eve as she wrapped the rings. She said she had second thoughts about giving them to me because she knew how special this ring was going to be and thought maybe I wanted to pick it out myself. As she sat down to wrap them, she was inspired to listen and write the note.

I put both rings on, one on each hand, so I could look at them. I went to a window so I could see them in the sunlight. I saw the fire in one and then the fire in the other. One was more blue, the other more green. I could no more choose which ring than Ahrynn could. So, I put them away and waited awhile.

A few hours later, I put the rings on again and tried to decide. Then I saw a scepter in one of the opals. It was perfect. The top of the scepter was round and orange in color, just like the sunrise in the morning. The tail of the scepter was full of all the colors of the chakra. The ring I chose was the ring Ahrynn was originally drawn to, the one that was "more her style." I was so excited about the scepter, I sat down next to Ahrynn and told her what happened. She said, "Opal is helping you." Without a doubt, this was the ring Opal wished to be part of.

It is now May. I haven't written about why Opal died, even though deep down I knew from her birth she was only here for a short while. In April, I asked not why she died, but rather how she died. I was told by Opal: "I left because it was time. I did not suffer, I just left my body. It was too small. Internally I did not have room for everything. I learned to stand, to play, I did everything the others did. They pushed me down, and I got up. You tried to help my physically at the end, but it was too uncomfortable. I didn't have room to digest my food, and my ribs were constricting my breathing, as you knew. My purpose had been served. My journey was complete. My purpose wasn't to overcome physical limitation, but rather to teach others not to judge. You tried to fix my leg physically; it didn't work, it wasn't meant to be. I was meant to have the physical limitation so you would learn, so you would connect, so I could communicate with you. I showed you how I could watch the others play all day then, in my sleep, I would do the same. In this way I never missed out. So, don't judge others thinking they are not fully experiencing life. I LIVED. I served my purpose, my journey was completed, so I left. I did not need to give you any signs or any time to help me go because part of my purpose was to show you that, when it is over, it is time to go, just that simple. As you have learned from other animals, in death there is a new beginning. Your Opal ring is a reminder to you every day that I live on, a reminder to not judge others. Remember, it is my purpose to be present with you as you journey on and complete your purpose."

Grow, Change, Endure and create moments that will last forever and always.
by Ahrynn McCann

CHAPTER 5

THE BLACKBIRD
Effortless Support

For the past two weeks, the blackbird has been hitting our window. Shade or sun, doesn't matter. He does this in the early morning before sunrise, in the middle of the day and at night.

Some family members speculated that he saw his reflection and thought it to be another male competing for a female. Others speculated he saw something shiny inside the house and wanted to get in. We figured whatever his reasoning for this behavior, it had to stop. So we hung a black sheet on the outside of the window, hoping this would stop his action and keep him from getting hurt. The blackbird figured out how to hang onto the sheet and still peck at the window. Very annoying, indeed.

Ahrynn, my daughter, called me on the way home from school and said she got the impression I was to sit outside with the bird and, when he tells us what he has to say, then he will leave. She said his message has something to do with two worlds or two times, conflict and that we need to acknowledge his presence.

So that is exactly what I am doing. Sitting on a stool by the window he is so determined to hit, waiting to see what he has to say.

As I waited in the stillness of the day, thoughts came into my head: *Protector, Guardian, Harmony. The sparrows have their nests and guard and protect them, yet we, the blackbirds, can live in harmony, share the same tree limbs, the same space.* Then the words *Reflection* and *Mirrored Image* came to mind. I closed my eyes and saw the outline of a bird coming toward me. I was told he wanted to take me somewhere, show me something. I became apprehensive because I have a mental block when it comes to visionary travels. Sensing this, he told me to go, in my mind, to my special place, put myself there. That I can do, and I did.

Then he flew out in front of me and asked me to watch him fly, to catch the air pockets that assist in lift, in effortless flight. He showed me I needed to allow myself to catch more lift to allow effortless support, not try to fight things so much, just float. The efforts of those around me will provide support and things will come together. (As I am writing this, four sparrows, two red-breasted males and two females, have perched on the fence very near to me and are just chatting away as if to share in this enlightenment, almost like a chorus to congratulate me on listening and understanding.)

I got tears in my eyes and thanked the blackbird for the message. But even then, I asked if this is what he came here for, what he wanted to say. I wanted to be sure I wasn't just thinking it. Intuitively, I was told *"Yes, this is my message; it is what I wanted to say."* I guess the struggle *is* the conflict.

I thanked him for the message and told him he didn't need to bang on the window anymore. We took the sheet down and he never returned. The annoying sound was gone; his message had been delivered.

Missing You

I miss you on the Holidays
The graduations, and the marriages to come
These will be the toughest of the days
I miss your smile, your laugh and your beliefs
I miss your humor, your Kleenexes
and your apartment key
I miss your Klondike barks and the goodies that were kept
The pill boxes and the one-a-days
Your Lucy slippers and great-granddads watch
Because I know it meant A lot
I miss looking back to watch you watch us
as we drove away
Knowing that we would be back on another day
I miss making you laugh
because I was the only one who could

I miss seeing the four generations of women
Standing side by side
But I know you are watching me grow
I know you were always scared
When the time came to let life go
But Mom was there, daughter and me
The elephants came to help you pass with ease
To be set free, fly away effortlessly
There is a gift in all of us, even though we may not believe
Through the guidance of others we are able to See
But even though you are with us
From each new sunrise to sunset
I can close my eyes and see you, a perfect silhouette

I think of you often
But most of all I will miss you
Always, Forever and throughout the Days

I Love You Great Nannie,
Your Great Grand Daughter

by Ahrynn McCann

A SPECIAL DEDICATION

Although this book is about animals, it would not be complete without the story of my grandmother's death. It is through her death that I was given a gift. The gift of the elephants. Her death process provided the opportunity to walk through a new door, to finally listen to that small, still voice.

When I was a child, I had dreams about elephants. I never understood the reason for the recurring dreams, but it was the same exact dream over and over. The elephants would come to my house asking for me. I hid in the closet until I thought it was safe. They found me and followed me through the field as I ran to my grandmother's house. I hid there, too. They asked for me and searched the house, so I ran again. I would wake from the dream with my heart beating fast, my palms sweaty, adrenalin rushing. I was scared. Why were elephants chasing me?

I married and had children of my own. The dreams still came. I shared this dream with my husband, knowing it was just a silly dream but not understanding why I kept having it.

When my grandmother died, THE DREAMS STOPPED! It was then and only then I realized the dreams were not to scare me. As a child, I thought I was being chased, when actually the elephants were only asking for me. When I would not answer, they had to follow me. They were persistent in their quest. It was during my grandmother's death process that I accessed the Energy of the Elephants, and the dreams stopped. They no longer needed to find me, I had finally answered.

I also find it interesting it was my grandmother's house I went to hide in, and it was at my grandmother's deathbed where the elephants found me.

DEATH IS A BLESSING. THANK YOU GRANDMA NAN FOR THE JOURNEY OF DEATH TOGETHER.

CHAPTER 6

THE BLESSINGS OF DEATH
(A Grandmothers' Passing)

On July 6, 2002, my mother called to give me advance warning that my Grandma Nan's health was rapidly deteriorating. She had been wanting to die for quite some time, and it seemed as though it might happen within the next few weeks. But the next day, Nan quickly took a turn for the worse. Mom called to let me know I might want to come over in the next few days to see her. I left the next morning.

On the drive over, I decided to turn off the radio and meditate about what I was to do. What could I do to help?

I asked my spirit guide, Michaela, to come, and she did. I felt her energy, as I always do when she is present. I asked her: "What am I to do?" She said, *"Do Reiki."* I replied, "Reiki is for healing, for moving energy to benefit one's well-being, to relieve pain." Michaela said, *"Exactly, you are using the Reiki energy to assist in minimizing her pain as she dies. You are using the energy to assist in making the dying process as effortless as possible."* Then she continued, *"Call upon the elephants, use their energy."*

I asked, "The elephants? But I don't know anything about elephants. Why elephants?"

Michaela replied, *"The elephants are your primary animal totem, call upon them in time of need to strengthen and heighten the Reiki."* Michaela also told me that when I arrived at my mom's house I needed to research the elephants and I would know when I found the right information.

My eyes filled with tears as I listened to what was being told to me. I could feel the energy within myself, and I knew this was an accurate, detailed message I was to follow. I did not question its validity; I knew it was a message from my guide.

I pulled into the driveway, turned off the car and, without taking any of my baggage, hurried to the front door. As usual, the door was locked. I knocked, and it seemed like forever before my mom answered the door. The first thing out of my mouth wasn't hello, or how are you, glad to see you;

rather, "I need to do some research on the internet on elephants." Surprised that I didn't want to chit-chat or go to see my Nan, my parents sensed my urgency and sat me down in front of the computer.

All I could think of for information sources were from my childhood when we watched television shows like *Mutual of Omaha's Wild Kingdom*. That didn't exist today, so I searched *Encarta* with the keyword "elephants." I could never have imagined what I was reading.

Elephants do not see well, but they have excellent hearing and sense of smell. As a group, they mourn the loss of one. If one is sick or dying, they all hover around together to support one another. They never leave one alone to die. Also, elephants communicate through vibration, sending or hearing the vibrational tone as far as a hundred miles away. I knew this was the information my spirit guide told me I would find.

With my research completed and the proper hellos to my parents, I went into Nan's room and sat beside her bed. Mom came in with me and stood on the other side. She told me what had happened over the past couple days with Nan's health. Nan had lost muscle control, could not open her eyes, speak, smile or move any of her limbs. Nan was without expression, yet alive and present. The hospice nurse had told Mom hearing is the last sense to go. After a short while, Mom left the room; it was just Nan and me together.

I held her hand and told her I was here, who I was and what a wonderful person she was. She was not a burden, we chose to help her and love her. I told her she was a very giving person, always thinking of others, never being selfish, and she had finally come to the end of her journey. Her time had come to close this life, and it was okay to leave her body. I shared with her that I was going to be a vessel and the Universe was going to be with us, to offer assistance in making her departure as painless as possible. I was going to use Reiki to move energy through her body, which would accelerate and smooth the dying process for her. We were going to call upon the elephants to assist with her departure.

Then I remembered my recent research. Elephants don't have good eyesight but they have excellent hearing and communicate through vibration. I remembered Michaela telling me to use the elephants' energy. I knew this vibrational tone was the energy to communicate with Nan. I was to use her ability to hear. How do I use the elephants' vibrations? What does it sound like, feel like? I did not know but trusted this, too, would be shown to me.

In the silence, we began our journey of death together. I put my hand on her chest and my other hand on her head. I asked that the white light of Christ surround us and the room, that all negative energy leave, as it was not welcome. I asked that only the energy and guides that were positive and willing to assist us come. I felt the energy move through my body and into Nan's. Then I asked that the elephants join us and allow us to use their energy to help Nan let go. As I pictured the elephant in my mind, I could feel a crowd. I told Nan we had many elephants joining us, not just one. I could feel their energy so intensely.

Without even thinking, I began to hum. My hum turned into a vibrational tone. I could feel the floor beneath me vibrate, the resonance of the vibration move up my feet, legs, trunk of my body, through my arms, hands and out my head. The wonderful, awesome part of this experience was that my hum was not my own. It was an extension of the vibration. And the most awesome of all was Nan began to make the exact same vibrational tone (hum). The woman who could not open her eyes, speak a word, grip a hand, was able to communicate with me on the exact same tone. I was elated at the energy of the elephants. I praised them and thanked them for their presence. When Nan quit vibrating, I stopped as well and continued with Reiki treatments. I did this for about an hour, then rested. I told her I would be back.

Around 11 p.m. I returned to Nan's room, rubbed her feet, massaged her legs and told her I loved her and she was a very special lady. Then I told her we were going to do the same thing over again. I was going to ask the Universe to use me as a vessel to channel healing energy and communicate through the elephants to ease her pain. The same thing happened as before, the vibration, the tone and Nan voicing the same tone. I ended with thanks to the Universe and to the elephants for the support they gave.

It was about midnight and my mom had already gone to bed. I noticed Nan was very hot to the touch underneath her body. The tops of her arms, hands, legs and forehead were normal temperature, but underneath she was burning up. I was concerned and not sure what to do, so I went upstairs and woke my mom and asked her to come help me roll Nan on her side.

During the next two hours, we cooled her down with wet towels and watched as she quickly transitioned from one stage of death to another. We called hospice three times within that two hours to let them know the changes we were experiencing. The nurse was mystified that things were progressing so quickly. Typically the process Nan was going through in two hours takes several days. I knew why; I wasn't mystified.

Nan had variations in breathing patterns, from short and irregular to gurgly and faint. She even had times when the breath would stop for a short time and start up again. Mom gave her morphine every fifteen minutes to help ease the pain and discomfort of her organs shutting down.

At 1 a.m. Nan was very comfortable. Her temperature was controlled, her breathing was now steady, soft and relaxed. Her face looked peaceful. The end was near. I sensed that the Reiki and elephant energy had comforted her, accelerated her stages of death and was now easing her pain to let go. Mom and I each took a hand and used lotion to massage her hands, wrist and forearms. As we rubbed her hands, I glanced at her once expressionless face and saw an expression of gratitude. The time had come and she was ready. Her expression was like when someone is surprised or excited. I could see it in her closed eyes and raised eyebrows. I thanked her and told her she was welcome.

As we continued to rub Nan's hands, I shared with Mom my experience with "Precious," my sheep who had died. I told her how I used Reiki to help her let go and die comfortably, and this is what the Universe did through me tonight. I told her Nan would not die or pass until we were not present. People and animals like to die without the loved ones next to them.

We assured Nan we were not leaving her, we would be across the hall in the living room on the hide-a-bed resting. We would not sleep, just listen for her and be there to comfort her. Mom had been playing a tape of the ocean/seagulls/rain she knew Nan liked. The hospice book said to play soft, relaxing music since they can hear and need comfort. So we did. We left her room at 2 a.m.

Mom was up after each song to check on Nan. We could hear her breathing along with the music. The music was soft enough that we could hear each breath she took. Her breathing was consistent, relaxed, unstrained, unlike earlier prior to the Reiki process when it was labored, erratic and strained. At the end of one song, Mom got up as usual to check and there was no breath. Sometime between 2:45 and 3 a.m. Nan stopped breathing. Mom asked me to come and confirm she was not breathing. I did. She was gone. She was so peaceful. We never heard a struggle, never heard a gasp; she was just gone. You could tell by the look on her face that she got her life-long wish, she "died in her sleep."

When by myself beside Nan's still, dead body, I thanked her for allowing me to share in this death process with her, for allowing me to be a vessel of the Universe, to call in the energy of the elephants, to confirm that the message I received from Michaela was so perfect and implemented with love, kindness and care. I thanked her for letting go and being in a better place -- free of pain, free of body bondage and having completed her journey, ready to move on.

Nan was not sick with cancer or any illness, she was not injured or had any trauma. She had decided life was too much of a struggle and she did not contribute to a meaningful, productive lifestyle and would rather die than continue. She chose to shut herself down. Six weeks prior to her death, I took her to the mall in a wheelchair. We shopped, purchased a book, *Chicken Soup for 65 and Older*, and a large-word crossword puzzle book. We ate hot dogs, pizza, Orange Julius®, cookies and candy. She was perfectly fine, could move her legs and feet to shuffle from behind the wheelchair to get to the bed and bathroom. She brushed her own teeth. It was amazing to me that someone could shut themself down so quickly.

After all the details of the nurse coming to confirm the death and the coroner taking Nan's body away, Mom and I knew we needed some nourishment and a chance to just breathe. We drove to a restaurant nearby and ordered breakfast. As we were waiting for our food to arrive, Mom said, "I have to ask you something. What were you doing in the room with Nan? Your father and I were watching television in the family room, and we could feel the floor vibrating. Curious, I got up, walked passed Nan's room and heard both you and Nan humming. I was shocked because I knew she couldn't speak or respond, but she was definitely humming."

In response to her question, I decided to take the opportunity to tell Mom about my spirit guide, that I knew her name. I had meditated on the way over, and Michaela told me what to do. I told her that's why, when I arrived, I insisted on getting on the internet to research elephants. I told her about the vibration of the elephants, about using Reiki to accelerate her death, to make her comfortable and as pain-free as possible. Mom was so pleased and at peace. She said she was so glad it didn't drag on for days and Nan did not suffer. Mom trusted what was happening, even though she didn't know and wasn't in the room with me. This conversation took my mother by surprise. I had never shared with her about Reiki or my experiences with the animals. Mom was content, she was not sure why she was, but just knew she was.

After breakfast, we stopped by the funeral home to make the arrangements and then went back home. My mom asked me to share with my father what I told her at breakfast. This opened up the door for me to share with both my mom and dad about Reiki, animal energy/totems and their role in our lives. It was a special time. Death brought us together in a different way. I thanked the Universe and Michaela for their assistance.

With most of the details taken care of, I started my two-hour drive back home. At the very location on the freeway where my spirit guide gave me instructions two days earlier, I heard a voice say, *"You were right, it's beautiful over here!"* I knew it was my grandmother. I began to cry. While she was alive, Nan and I always debated whether one died and stayed in the grave until the resurrection or if the soul left the body and went to Heaven – "the other side," as some call it. Nan believed one stayed in the ground until resurrected. I always told her when she found out, let me know. This was Nan's way of telling me now she knows and I was right.

To this day, I always respect a moment of silence when I travel through that special spot on the freeway. I am reminded of the message so perfectly given from my guide and the message so perfectly sent from my grandmother. I feel her energy and her presence. Through my grandmother's death, I received the blessing of experiencing the process of death, how the one dying can leave us a gift, open another door, and start a new journey.

My grandmother's death opened the door to the elephant energy. Her death, our journey together, allowed me to be a vessel, to experience an energy that would be a gift for me to use on my journey with animals. I now knew, without question, the power of elephant energy and its effectiveness in death.

On July 18, as I was climbing into bed, I heard my grandmother's voice. I had just settled in and pulled the covers up over me when I was startled, or should I say I took notice of a thought in my head that said, *"So, I see you stuck me in the corner and just left me there. I see nothing's changed."* I immediately knew it was my grandmother. It sounded just like something she would say. What she was referring to is I placed her urn of ashes in the corner of the dining-room table. The table is a corner bench unit with a corner shelf just the perfect size for the urn. We took a candle off to put the urn there. I replied, "No, we didn't just leave you in the corner and ignore you. You are in the corner of the dining room table, which is the center of all activity. We eat there, the children do their homework there. You are not in a closet or hidden somewhere. Besides, you aren't dead, you are very much alive. Your ashes are just the physical part that remains, so what does it matter to you anyway?" She replied, *"Just noticed."*

I began to cry tears of joy. This was so wonderful that Nan had come to see me so soon. I knew she would. The words she spoke, whether she truly meant them or not, she knew I would recognize as hers, for this is how she was in her active life here, very cynical and sarcastic. I didn't mistake it at all. I was overjoyed. I called my mom and shared the experience.

*Live with an open mind and allow for change.
We resist change in most areas of our lives
because we fear the unknown.
It is the unknowns, that the universe is guiding us
back to where we need to be in our journey through life.*

by Ahrynn McCann

CHAPTER 7

THE PRESENT ISN'T ALWAYS JUST NOW
(As Told By Pepper)

This morning as I drove to work, in my mind I saw Pepper, my seventeen-year-old German short-hair dog. I acknowledged her presence, and she said she had something to say. Here is what she told me:

"When we think of the present moment or 'being present,' sometimes we need to think of 'the present' as being broader than 'just this moment.' What you think of as a long time, in Universe time, is merely a fraction of time.

"When we think of the 'present,' it can be the Present Path we are on or the Present Process of Change, with PROCESS being our new present time. If we have decided to make a change in career, family, location, etc., this change represents a new path -- a new present. Within this present (path or direction), we can have times or moments when we are very 'present' or focused and achieve much. We can also have times when we are 'not so present or focused' and we seem to stand still. Take, for example, what I have been trying to show you in these, my last days of life (at least you think I am in my last days).

"I told you five months ago it was time for me to go. I am still here. You thought I was to go within a few days, but it only meant my present path of the last part of my life had begun, it was time to start the final stage of my journey. During this time, I have days when I am at the top of my game; I am bouncy, barking, ears up, face lit up, prance, run and explore. Other days, I am lost, confused and can't find my way out of the barn, can't find the water bucket and even fall into the pool. Some days I don't even recognize you or your voice. I am even startled at your very presence. There are days when I can't get enough to eat and days when I don't eat at all. This doesn't mean I am not dying and not on my present path of being in the final stage of my life. This is to show you that, even while in your present path or journey, you will have days of great accomplishments and days of setbacks.

"My good days and bad days don't mean I am going to live longer or die sooner. It is just to show you that the present is a particular part of the JOURNEY, with many present moments of challenges. A choice to take a path sets that path in motion while you can still be living in a different present moment. Therefore, it might appear the present moment (i.e., my good days) changes my intention to be on a certain path (the final stage of my life) when, in fact, it doesn't -- I am still dying, just not today. You can decide today that you are going to take or start a certain journey that will happen in six months, one year or three years and know your present journey IS (includes) the 'process of change.' The Complete Change (six months, one year, etc.) is in itself a journey, a present time.

"I told you I must leave in order to help you write. But you see, I am helping you write even before I am gone. You saw me in your thoughts, you acknowledged my presence, and look at the story you have written. I wanted you to feel my presence and know we can communicate before I leave. Remember when you tried to help me pass on a month ago and I wouldn't? I kept getting up and leaving while you were trying to assist me; well, now you know why, I haven't finished my job here yet. It is time to go, it just wasn't time to go that day. It is time for me to pass on -- just not today. You had decided you would find out later why it didn't work, the energy of the elephants, to help me pass. It wasn't that the energy of the elephants didn't work, it does, it is just that it was in conflict with MY journey, the journey I was to take to help you.

"You understood at the time that there was a reason for my not passing and you did not let it bother you or weigh you down with second guesses that maybe you didn't do something right. Now you know why. Always trust the outcome of your intentions and your work, as the Universe knows all and is assisting in your journey as well.

"Do you remember when you would sit with me and want to communicate and you just couldn't get anything? You were told earlier you and I would communicate, so you would try and be disappointed. We are communicating, you just needed to be at a point in your journey when you could see my journey as well. You heard me very easily today, and it will get even easier for us, even when I am gone, for I will always be with you.

There will be more before I go. I have much to share."

It was Thursday, May 27, and I was getting the message from Pepper that she was ready to go. Even though I was doing my best to keep her comfortable, and even though she did not complain or appear to be in pain (she was alert, still running and playing, getting in and out of the swing on her own, eating four meals a day, etc.), she was tired of being in her old body.

We sat on the swing, just the two of us, and said our goodbyes. I called in the energy of the Universe and the elephants, just as before. After a short while, I notice her relaxing and her heart rate slowing. Then, all of a sudden, her upper lip started to quiver and look snarley, like she was going to bite someone. Saliva started foaming at her mouth and dripping onto my leg. She stuck her legs straight out and was trembling.

I immediately stopped the process and started to calm and massage her. She responded quickly, stabilized, jumped down out of the swing and ran over to the old garden area and wandered around as if nothing had happened.

I could not believe my eyes. This was so reminiscent of earlier in the year when I sat at the barn and tried to let her go then but it didn't work. I didn't keep trying like before. I remembered what Pepper said later, that she couldn't go that day because she hadn't finished her job yet.

Pepper finally laid down in the grass and I sat with her. I got the impression she had something to say, but I could not put myself in the right connection with her. Not wanting to struggle with mind-chatter clutter, I decided to once again ask for the assistance of a spirit guide in communicating with Pepper.

As before, Pepper was laying on the cool, green grass just as content as could be. Through the spirit guide, Pepper said she has had a good life and, yes, it was time to go. She thought she would be able to help me with my journey and go without veterinary assistance, that she would offer herself for me to practice using the elephant's and universal energy, but she found it just too hard. She was having difficulty letting go of this world and us. She was ready, her body was ready, but the goodbye part was just too difficult. She started to leave and then fought it. She would miss the dogs, the other animals, the home, and me. She asked that I make her comfortable, that she would like assistance in leaving and she wanted everyone there.

It made sense now why she would always have the seizures, she was fighting leaving, she was feeling herself go and didn't want to. I made the appropriate phone calls to schedule the euthanasia but the veterinary offices were already closed for the holiday weekend — Memorial Day. Pepper would have to wait a few more days. The morning of June 2 I called the veterinarian, and they scheduled us for a ranch visit the same day at noon.

Talk about difficult! I knew it wouldn't be hard to actually have Pepper put to sleep, but what I didn't realize was knowing she only had three more hours to live would be very difficult. She was laying in the grass, chewing on a bone while I was making the arrangements for her departure. She would hold her head up high, ears up and just looked like she was a healthy dog. She didn't look like a dog that only had three hours to live. I knew it was what she wanted, but watching the clock tick down minute by minute was very difficult.

A few last details needed to be taken care of: The children needed to be called so they could be there, too, to say their goodbyes. I stopped the project I was working on and waited for Pepper to finish her bone. Then, once again, we went and sat in the swing together, just she and I. We talked about things, how we purchased her from the animal shelter and immediately took her to the childrens' school to show them our new family member. I remembered the big smiles on their faces. We didn't know her name, so we just kept calling out names until something sounded right – Pepper seemed to get a response. She became a part of our lives and enriched us. I talked to her about bringing up the other dogs and teaching them not to go past the gate and general manners. I told her that when she was gone, Two-Bitts, our black Lab, and I would still sit in the swing and she would probably be "whoo-whooing" from the tree above us. That she would always be with us.

Two-Bitts

Kylle

I just sat with Pepper, stroked her and loved her. Kylle, our dalmation, and Two-Bitts each came over on their own and licked her on the face, as if they were saying their goodbyes as well. Reggie, our Jack Russell, just stayed in the distance, as he was never allowed to come into the space at the swing (an arrangement the dogs came up with and all seemed to honor).

As the stroking hour of noon fast approached, the children arrived from work and school. My husband and the dogs, Kylle, Two-Bitts, and Reggie, were there, too.

When the veterinarian arrived, Michael brought her to the backyard to join all of us already gathered around Pepper. Kylle didn't make a peep or a bark, he didn't show any signs of protection. Two-Bitts decided to leave the circle and go over by the bushes along the fence. He was still within "being present" range, just not in the immediate circle. I figured that was where he wanted to be and so it was. Kylle and Reggie were very close to the swing and neither had a fit about Reggie's close presence. It was okay this time, as this was a special occasion and everyone had been summoned by Pepper to be there.

We spoke to the vet for a moment, and she said she would be injecting a large dose of anesthesia at a slow rate and Pepper would just fall asleep. She asked if we had all said our goodbyes and if we were ready. We were.

Pepper laid with her front legs across my lap and her bottom in the swing. I told her she was finally on her way and she must go in order for her to complete her journey. I told her everyone was here, just as she had wanted. The vet started to inject the fluid into her front leg. Pepper started letting go, her head relaxing and falling into my arms. She just went to sleep. I let the others know as she went. She never twitched, it was very peaceful. The vet did an excellent job. I shed a few tears as she left, but I was so happy for Pepper. This was the only way she could move on.

The dogs were awesome. It amazed me how the dogs placed themselves in Pepper's presence, how they said their goodbyes. They just sat there, didn't bother anyone for attention, didn't play with one another, they were just present. Pepper must have been talking to them as well.

Pepper taught me so much. She even allowed me to learn that not all of us have an easy time leaving. Even though I have been given the gift from the Universe of allowing myself to be a channel for assisting animals to leave, not all of them (or humans, for that matter) will be able to, and that it is not a reflection on my ability to effect a successful departure. The animal must be willing to go. Then I thought back upon my other animals. Precious, our

sheep, left us before I knew how to assist with the departure. Hope and Gina, both goats, allowed me to assist with both of their departures, which were peaceful. Gina, however, was similar to Pepper, in that she took three days to go and even told me she liked this place and wasn't in a hurry to leave. Pepper gave me the gift of her wanting to be of service for my benefit, yet, in the end, she had a difficult time leaving and fought all the way. I understood, and even in this she taught me that it wasn't my inability to connect with the Universe, it was her unwillingness to leave us.

Pepper and I spent a lot of time in the swing together. We would just sit and swing and enjoy the closeness. Usually Two-Bitts, the black Lab, would sit with us, with me in the middle and the two of them on each side. We were just present with one another. As Pepper said, she had her good days and bad days. Her halter was left on so during the bad days we could guide her along if needed, keep her from falling into the pool or use it to pull her out of the pool if she fell in. It was not a hardship; it was a joy for us to help her, because she gave us so much joy.

If it were our decision, we would have kept Pepper with us until she died of natural causes. But this wasn't our decision, it was Pepper's. Listening to her wishes, respecting the she does have a journey of her own, we knew that this, too, was important for us to understand. Pepper left us on June 2, 2004. It was a beautiful day. Even though she didn't look ill, she was ready to go. But I know Pepper will always be present, and I look forward to her communications.

*Find that sacred place within yourself,
it is the most powerful, invigorating, peaceful place
in your deepest heart of hearts
that remains untouchable for anyone or anything
to take away from you.*
　　　　　　by Ahrynn McCann

CHAPTER 8

ALL POWER COMES FROM WITHIN

It was weaning season, the time when all the mom goats were in the front pasture, babies in the back, with an empty pasture in between. Bellows could be heard day and night, mom's calling babies and babies calling moms. It's a pitiful sound. Nonetheless, it has to be done.

Rescue, one of the goats, got her name because we "rescued" her from death. We bought her at public auction for $27.50. In comparison, a healthy goat would sell for $130. She couldn't walk and was very near death. She had obviously been starved, malnourished and left for dead. Skinny as could be, not an ounce of meat or muscle on her, her hips were broken down, legs so thin she could hardly walk. When she walked, it seemed as though you could see her thinking about every step and how it hurt. We nursed her along, gave her all the fine amenities an animal could want and promised her she would stay here and have the good life until she died. She would never be sold or given away.

Rescue was one of the moms being separated from the babies. It had only been a week since the separation, and Rescue was having a difficult time adjusting. She had become so thin and wouldn't eat, she didn't have an appetite, lacked ambition and didn't have the desire to even exist. Rescue had given birth to triplets. These babies were her entire life. She was an excellent mom, letting them nurse as often as they wanted for as long as they wanted. She existed for them and they were spoiled. We knew it would be hard on her to be separated, but they were older now and dragging her down from the constant nursing. Figuring she was lonesome for her babies, we decided it didn't matter -- we either let the babies drag her down or she starves herself and dies of a broken heart.

The easiest solution was to move Rescue to the back pasture. She would be the only mom with all the babies. As I opened the gate from the first pasture, Rescue seemed to become more aware and alert. She knew she was getting closer to her babies. When I opened the gate to the back pasture, she just knew her babies were there somewhere. Being so weak yet anxious, Rescue didn't have the strength to go searching for her babies. She could smell them. Her nose was twitching, her legs were dancing with excitement. I went and found her babies and brought them to her. She was so pleased to see them and, even though it had been a week, they knew she was their mom. Rescue's heart must have been singing with joy. She smelled and nudged each one, licked their faces and checked them over from head to tail, all the while assuring them they would be together. Within a day, Rescue started to do more, stand more, eat more and move around. Within three days, she was running from feeder to feeder and grazing all day.

Then, all of a sudden, she fell off weight again – she was weak, stumbling as she walked, selective in what she ate, and ate very little at that. So we started antibiotics and baby food (rice cereal with fresh mashed bananas and blue/green algae). She wouldn't eat on her own, so I used a turkey baster to feed her. Sucking up a full syringe of mush, I put my fingers between her lips, slipped the baster to the back of her jaw and slowly dispensed the mush. She seemed to like the feedings and even chewed the tip of the baster a bit. I also syringed water with vitamins and electrolytes several times a day.

We had to carry Rescue out to the field and place her in the shade and then move her as the shade moved, as she could not stand and support her own weight. Her babies would come over to see her, give her snoodles, lay in the shade next to her for awhile then go off to play with the others. They were sure to come back often to check in with Mom.

Within a few days, Rescue began to selectively eat again. Leaves are what she wanted, and only mulberry leaves. It was difficult to feed her a special diet with all the other animals around. Goats always believe the other goat has something better. So we were forced to move Rescue and her babies into the corral where we could feed her without the bother of the other goats. She had lost the ability to stand or even the strength to get up on her front knees. I figured as long as she had the desire to eat, we had a chance. A shade shelter made of a tarp and T-posts attached at one end to the top rails of the board fence was erected for her to lay under. All she could do was shift her weight to lay on one side or the other. Her spirit was strong, her will to survive enormous, and a look of thanks was in her eyes.

I got up every morning before work to syringe water and liquid diet down Rescue's throat. I lifted her hind quarters so she could stand on her rear legs and kneel on her front legs. Once steady, I lifted her chest so she could stand on all fours. Her left front leg was crippled, not allowing her to take any steps, just stand. All we did was stand, a little at a time; one minute, then three minutes, then five minutes, and so on. I did the same routine in the evening. On weekends, I helped her to stand several times a day. I didn't want her muscles to atrophy. Her babies went back and forth. They spent time with Mom in the corral then went out to play with the others. Even though Rescue couldn't let them nurse anymore, she was attentive to them and enjoyed their company.

I had prepaid for attending a Spirituality Day in Sacramento on June 1. Rescue's illness made me reconsider my plans. She needed attention, and I had mixed emotions about attending the classes, which I knew would be wonderful but required me to be away for the entire day. I felt like I was neglecting Rescue to do something for myself. Finally, overcoming my uneasiness, I went to Sacramento and attended three classes, learning about auras, the shamanic journey and developing psychic skills.

In the first class I kept drifting, my thoughts wondering about Rescue, was she doing okay, sad I was not there to assist her, which meant she had to lay in the same place all day. The second class, the shamanic journey, was excellent. It was explained that a shamanic journey is one in which we "hunt" out our fears in order to challenge and conquer or banish those fears. It is in conquering fear that we succeed and move forward in our journey. The class included a meditation in which we were to be met by an animal that would take us to a certain place where we would then be told something of value and then must, in turn, help something before returning from that place.

At the beginning of the meditation, the instructor placed a card in our hands, one of the seven Laws of the Shamans. Mine read "All Power Comes From Within." I immediately welled up in tears and Rescue came to mind. I tried to remain composed as the instructor was beginning the guided meditation. I, of course, was preoccupied with my own emotions and did not succeed in following the meditation, but I did succeed in hearing Rescue's message. As the class continued to follow the instructor's directions, I continued to follow Rescue's energy.

Rescue told me her being crippled was to show me I am crippling myself by taking on too much, too much work, too much family, too much trying to do it all. And the selective eating was to show me I must be selective in what work I choose to take on. Don't take everything, select a few; the easy, the needy, the long-time client, it didn't matter why, just be selective. I was astonished. In the quietness of the classroom, I couldn't follow the meditation, but I was able to open the channel of communication and hear Rescue's message meant just for me.

When I returned home that evening, it was already dark. I had been away all day in classes and was anxious to spend time with Rescue, so I went straight down to the pasture. Michael had moved Rescue from the corral out to the prairie for the day. Since she couldn't walk, Rescue was still there. I took a chair with me and sat down next to her. I told her, "I got your message loud and clear." I thanked her for sending it to me, for being an example to get my attention. I let her know that, since I got her message and understood her message, it was okay for her to get better. I fed her, gave her water (by syringe) and just sat with her. I reached my arms over her back and under her belly to stand her up and help her walk. I grasped her left front ankle with my hand to keep it from crippling and I became her fourth leg. I crawled alongside her on the prairie grass to be that extra leg. I didn't care if I crawled in feces (and I did) or if my knees got sore or poked by stickers.

We only walked a few steps; that's all she had strength for. It was a long way to the barn and, at this pace, we wouldn't make it. It was going to be a cool evening and I didn't want her out in the cold air -- her immune system wasn't strong enough, too risky of getting pneumonia. I stood her up once again and told her I needed her help. I was going to carry her to the barn and she would have to work with me.

It was well into the night, no one else was around, just me and Rescue. I asked the Universe (guides and angels) to help me carry this 100-pound goat. I wrapped my left arm at the base of her neck around her chest and my right arm under her tail. I just lifted. It was so easy, no strain, as if she was placed in my arms. Then, as requested, Rescue did her part, she turned her neck and wrapped her head around my left arm toward my back to offer counterbalance. We got to the barn in no time at all, light as a feather. I thanked Rescue and the Universe.

The next day, we put Rescue back in the corral under the shade tent to feed. I reminded her I would make changes so I wasn't crippling myself and I would be selective. I thanked her again for the message. I spent the next ten days, one or two hours every morning and night, getting her special food, helping her stand and walk. I could see the determination in her eyes. She would fall over and over again but not give up. Many times the fall sent her nose-first into the ground, but she just shook it off, ready to try again.

As I was sitting with Rescue, an intuitive thought came into my mind that she needed magnesium to help strengthen her muscles. I had just read articles about magnesium and decided to give it a try. I crushed 500 mg each morning and night, mixed it with water and syringed it down her throat. I gave her a banana each morning and night, and she loved them, peelings and all. We later added almonds from our tree and rose petals from the rose garden. She and I became so bonded that when she saw me, she would call to me like a mother calls her baby goats. If I left, she called to me.

During this time, I began to put into practice the things I learned from Rescue about being selective and not crippling myself. In response, Rescue began to stand longer, determined once again to walk. When she saw me coming, she would start getting herself into position, anticipating that I would be getting her up to stand and walk. It was as if she was going out to play. Each day got better.

By the seventh day, Rescue was getting herself up on all fours, more sound and stable, not wavering. She actually, for the first time in many days, regurgitated and chewed like a goat should. I knew we were getting better now. On day eight, figuring she was ready for new scenery and interaction, Rescue was reunited with all the other goats. I tried to help her to the barn and still be her fourth leg, but she was going so fast I was afraid she would stumble. I told her to slow down, I couldn't crawl that fast. This was the farthest she had walked since her illness began. I put her in the corral at night only to feed her the special leaves so the others wouldn't trample her and eat it all. The mulberry leaves seemed to be doing the trick. I fed her in the morning as well, then opened the gate so she could graze with the others.

By the ninth day, Rescue was running again, butting heads with other goats, no longer crippled and wanting to be with the herd. By day ten, she no longer needed the special diet. She didn't call for me as much, but I knew we would always share a special bond.

Even though Rescue is not crippled anymore, whenever I see her, I will always ask myself "Am I crippling myself today?" She is my daily reminder that truly "ALL POWER COMES FROM WITHIN." Her power to live, to struggle and take on adversity to deliver a message and become well again to teach me truly came from within.

*Respect the beauty that lays deep within
the most honest and peaceful part of your soul.
For it is when we see Our own beauty
through Our eyes that we are then able
to give that peaceful Beauty to others.*

by Ahrynn McCann

CHAPTER 9

LOOK AROUND!!

It was a nice day, not too hot, not too cool. Just right for taking a llama on a walk. We have several llamas, but Jack is the one that is a real walker. He likes his pack harnessed across his back and cinched tight under his belly. He carries his pack with great pride, assuming he is being of service to someone.

Jack enjoys going out and about. He is easy to catch in the field. Actually, I wouldn't call it "catching" by any means. All I do is grab the halter and lead rope from the hook on the barn wall and, with both in hand, walk out wherever he is. Unlike other types of animals or even other llamas, for that matter, he will just stand and watch me get closer. He might turn around or take a few steps away, but that's all. If I tell him we are going on a walk, he stands perfectly still. I slip the halter on his head, fasten it, attach the lead rope and off we go. Jack usually gives a few looks over his shoulder to the others as he is led away, as if to tell them, "I'll be back."

Although today was a perfect day for a walk, it was a disaster getting Jack to cooperate. It was so uncharacteristic of him. As usual, I had planned ahead. The trailer was hitched to the truck, and I had checked all the connections and lights. With lead rope and halter in hand, I opened the gate and went into the field to get Jack. I tried for twenty minutes or better, but he evaded me at every attempt. He ran away, he ignored my call, he hid from me by sandwiching himself between two other llamas. He just wouldn't listen.

Finally, out of frustration, I decided Jack would have to get caught the old-fashion way – by use of the catch pen. Our catch-pen was large enough to contain twenty-plus goats or sheep, with a large swinging gate at either end. It had a squeeze chute that turned and rotated for ease in trimming goat's and sheep's feet. It had a water trough, feeders and shade. Quite the setup for special occasions, and this was one of them.

Now that Jack was stirred up, on high alert and aware of my frustration, I figured the easiest way to get his attention and cooperation was with food – sweet cob, that is! This molasses and corn mixture is sweet like candy, sticky, too. I opened the barn door, reached into the grain barrel and scooped up a bucket full of sweet cob. As the door closed behind me, the llamas had already picked up the scent of the grain and were anxiously watching to see where I was going. By the time I started dumping the grain into the feeders in the catch pen, they were right beside me. I closed the gate behind them and watched as they enjoyed their treat.

When they were almost finished savoring their treat, all I had to do was slip Jack's halter on, snap the lead rope to the clip, load and go. I opened the gate to the pen, and quickly closed it behind me. As the other two llamas neared the gate, I opened it just enough for them to get through, figuring it would be easier if Jack didn't have others to hide behind, but somehow Jack snuck by with them. Thoroughly frustrated by now, Jack was back out in the field, and I gave up.

My daughter Ahrynn and I had planned on going on the walk together. She had been at the house getting some last-minute things together for the walk and came down to the pen just as it all ended. I told her what had happened, how Jack had escaped my attempts and that we just weren't meant to go on a walk today.

I suggested maybe Jack would get spooked on the trail or we might have mechanical problems with the trailer. All I knew is Jack was never that elusive, so he must have sensed something. As we accepted the fact we weren't going on a walk, we closed the gates and turned to walk away. That's when I noticed Gina, a goat, was still in the catch-pen, minding her own business, out of the way in a corner. This was a surprise. I was so focused on the llamas and the catch, I didn't even notice Gina was in the pen with us. More importantly, GINA WAS IN LABOR.

This was a total surprise. Gina wasn't even close to being due. She was hardly even showing a bulging belly, she hadn't dropped yet, nor did she have a milk bag. She was several months out. I knew this was going to be a touchy delivery.

Ahrynn quickly got some hot, soapy water, towels and alcohol. When she returned, I told her this is the reason we didn't go on our walk and Jack knew it. He knew Gina was in trouble, and he needed me to stop focusing on him and focus on her.

Gina knew we were there to help her, and she followed us to the barn where we could tend to her delivery better. We could tell she didn't want to be alone; she already knew things weren't right and she wouldn't be able to do this delivery on her own. Gina wasn't dilated, so I did Reiki, a type of hands-on healing therapy, in an attempt to help her dilate so we could deliver. Gina seemed receptive, and we could feel the energy flowing. I could tell she was having difficulty. Her drainage was a brownish-yellow color, and I knew we had problems – that was a sign of death and decay.

I soaped my hands and arms all the way up to the elbows and attempted to reach in and assist in stretching the cervix. We contacted the veterinarian and they advised under the circumstances to give her fifteen minutes. If no delivery, bring her in.

By this time, Gina was getting exhausted and I needed her alert and pushing. I managed to get the baby in the canal with a few pushes, but only one foot was showing. It was a back foot, which presented an even more difficult birth. A few more pulls and pushes, and the leg was extended. I knew immediately the baby was dead. The leg was swollen, hairless and full of fluid. I could not deliver this baby without compromising Gina's health.

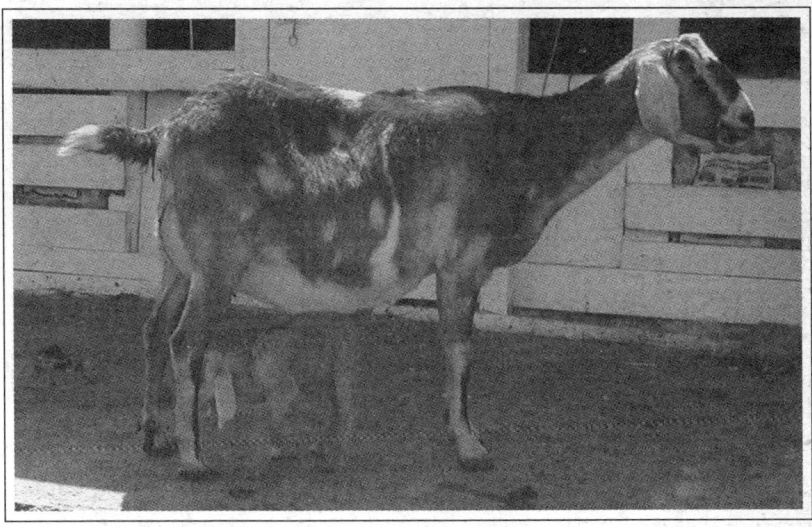

The trailer was already hitched and ready to go. With what strength Gina had left, we loaded her in the trailer, and off we went to the veterinarian. They took one look and knew the baby was dead and the only way to complete the abortion/delivery was to put Gina under anesthesia. She was too weak to push and still not dilated enough for a delivery. I watched as they restrained Gina in a comfortable position and slipped the anesthesia mask over her nose. Her eyes became droopy and I could see her body relaxing. Somehow,

I think she sensed all would be fine, it was almost over. Afterwards, the doctor told us the baby had been dead for at least 48 hours; it was a male. Gina survived just fine.

Jack

The lesson Gina and Jack taught me was to not be frustrated with a situation that isn't working. Don't struggle, don't force it to happen. Let it go and look to see what it is you are supposed to be seeing. I was so focused on getting Jack haltered that even when Gina was in the pen with us, I didn't notice her needs. Even in my frustration that I couldn't catch Jack, I realized there was a reason for it, *I just had to look!*

Upon my return from the veterinarian's office, I went to the pasture to see Jack. He came right up to me and stood still, just like he always did. I told him

I wanted to thank him for not letting me catch him. Had we left together, Gina would have been by herself, with no one to help. Given the length of time we would have been gone, Gina would have died giving birth to an already dead baby. Jack knew, and I thanked him for his sacrifice of the walk so I would pay attention somewhere else. I kissed him and hugged him.

Gina provided yet another lesson for me. She is always by herself, always getting butted, always an outcast. She chooses to eat by herself, stay away from the herd, sleep by herself, a real loner. I was at the barn just before dark and she was already in the stall in the corner by herself. I knelt down beside her, stroked her neck and back and asked her why she was always alone, by herself, not socializing. In the silence that followed, this thought came to mind: *"She is a loner to show me I need to spend more time by myself, just sitting in the field like she does, away from everything so I may look upon the herd, absorb my surroundings and become more aware."* Tears came to my eyes, I hugged Gina and thanked her for the example she set.

The next day, I looked out into the field and saw Gina had joined the herd! Now I must learn to do as she did. What an awesome teacher she is. I need time alone to ponder, to reflect, to allow the Universe to speak. This is part of my new journey.

This experience reminded me of a book I had been reading on animal totems. The author stated that each animal is for a different purpose. Some come to teach us patience, forgiveness, love, temperance and other things. We must LOOK at what each one has to offer and learn from them. I guess Gina was teaching me to LOOK AROUND.

*To gain Courage in your heart,
you must first have the Courage to grow!*
by Ahrynn McCann

CHAPTER 10
GET ON WITH OUR DREAMS

My father had back surgery, so every couple days, I traveled from my house to my parents', a two-hour drive each way, to help my mom during the surgery and recovery. This schedule continued for two weeks.

Between coming and going, it seemed as if the only time I had to spare was for a quick walk through the pasture to pet and say hello to each of the animals. During one of these quick walks, I remember spending time with the llama and donkey and seeing Rescue, our goat, at the barn. Knowing this was a sign she might not be feeling well, I yelled over to her, "Rescue, don't you go getting sick now. I don't have the time nor the energy for it."

Over the years, Rescue's pattern was to give birth and then, about two months later, be sick, weak and unable to walk or graze. She wasn't like the other moms. She allowed her babies to nurse as often and as long as they wanted. She enjoyed being a mom, even if it meant she became sick.

I had finally finished traveling back and forth to help care for my dad and thought I would go to the prairie and spend some time with Rescue, check in with her to see how she was doing. When I saw her, I realized she had ignored my command a week earlier about not getting sick. It seemed as though it didn't matter to her that I didn't have the time or the energy, she was going to make sure I spent the time with her now.

Even though Rescue went through this process every birthing season, because she was so ill when we purchased her, it seemed as though each occurrence was more difficult to get through; more complications and a longer recovery. As before, she was unable to walk and graze. But she was alert and had a healthy appetite.

As I sat with Rescue, stroking her long, black neck, rubbing the sides of her nose just below her eyes, I couldn't help but wonder if this was all she had the energy for, the last round. I wanted to be sure Rescue knew how much joy she had given us being part of our family. She and I had communicated together, she provided stories and lessons for the book, and she was a companion to many. She owed us nothing. I assured her Sweetie (another goat) would take her babies in and they would play with Sweetie's babies just as they were doing now. I asked Rescue to let me know her intentions.

The next evening, in my dreams, I saw Rescue standing firm and strong. It was like a flash. It startled me and I woke up. I figured she had died and was letting me know she was strong and well now on the other side. I did not feel impressed to jump up out of bed, get dressed and race down to the barn. I was at peace, with no sense of urgency. I quickly fell back to sleep. A few hours later, the sunrise glared through our bedroom window and woke me up. It was time to get up and tend to business with Rescue.

Figuring Rescue had died but not wanting it to be true, I grabbed mulberry leaves to take with me, just in case. My stomach was queasy. Even though I am comfortable with animals dying or passing on, it is still an anxious moment just before you actually know did they pass on or not. Instead of waiting until I got right up close to her, I started looking for signs of life before I got there.

From a distance, I could see her neck curled back against her belly, a typical position in sleeping and death. As I approached, I didn't see any breathing, her rib cage was still, her lips were apart and her eyes were slits. She definitely looked dead. I knelt down beside her, swished the flies from her nose and mouth, stroked her face and told her she looked peaceful and I was glad she didn't struggle and just let go. Then SHE MOVED!! I jumped back and fell off my knees. I was so surprised! She opened her eyes, lifted her head and immediately began eating the leaves in my hand.

I told Rescue the story of what happened, my startling picture of her standing strong. Now that she wasn't dead, I figured she sent me the picture to let me know she wanted to live. She was alert, anxious to get up and around, even though she still couldn't fully support her own weight. I guess I got my answer. Before leaving to return to the house, I helped her stand for a few minutes.

With everyone else still asleep, I decided to sit down and read a little. Several months earlier I had started reading a book by Susan Chernack McElroy, *Heart in the Wild*. For some reason, I thought to pick this book up and browse through it. The next chapter where I had left off reading was on Dream Master. This intrigued me, since I had just been having dreams about Rescue and knew this was the chapter I should read.

Susan was talking about how our journey and life purpose is our dream, something we bring with us at birth. She continued by saying we tend to let that purpose slide, let other things become important and lose sight of the dream. Susan also stated in this chapter that a "…dream is tenacious, it will always and endlessly send messengers, something dressed as a friend or an interesting stranger…" In Susan's experience, it was a little kitten that came into her life for a brief couple of hours and had "called her back to her dream and would never let her forget it again."

In my case, Rescue was once again my messenger. She had brought me the message "Power Comes From Within" the last time she was down and out. This time, she wanted me to stop stalling and get back to my dream, to get on track, to get back to writing my book about animals.

I put the book down, made Rescue's dinner blend and went out to tell her: "I got the message, again." I told her I would begin writing (which I did that very night) and would stop putting everything else (work, household, others, etc) in front of it. I told her she sent the message loud and clear, and I was sorry she had to endure the suffering again to get my attention. She tried telling me weeks before when I saw her at the barn and told her I didn't have time or energy for her to get sick, but that didn't matter. I had a reawakening to experience, a journey to get on with. Rescue is so selfless, and her purpose is to keep me on track. As I laid in bed that night ready to fall asleep, I told Rescue I wrote and thanked her for the message.

Rescue had once again delivered her message to me, it was time for her to get better. She had done her job, got my attention, and she could now move on. Each time I went down to see Rescue, she was anxious and excited, moving around, scooting her legs in a hurry to get up, only to realize she still couldn't get up on her own. I knew she was wanting to participate in the activities with the other goats and her babies.

In between feedings, I rubbed her face, kissed her nose and we exchanged breaths. I would put my nose to her nose and breathe out. She would breathe in, taking my breath with hers. Then she did the same for me. It's our way of sharing, of being close. Tonight, we looked into each others eyes very deeply and saw our souls and knew we had shared something very special.

It has only been a couple days since I got Rescue's message. Some days she seems strong, trying to stand on her own, and other days she can't even help us get her up. With all this back and forth -- strong one day, weak the next -- I pondered why Rescue was hanging on. She is much stronger, more alert, putting on weight more so than a week ago, yet why is she not standing strong? What is the purpose in going through all these days of laying around, what life is that? I have yet to learn from Rescue why she is hanging on in this state of existence.

Once again, I was abruptly awakened in the morning by a dream. Rescue was not only up and standing, she was frolicking, bucking, leaping about the prairie, as if to say "Look at me, I'm all better now!" I was elated!

I jumped up out of bed, quickly got dressed in whatever was handy and ran to the barn. Rescue had moved herself quite a ways from where I had left her the night before. By the time I had finished feeding her, my husband, Michael, had wandered down to the barn. We picked Rescue up to stand. She was moving her front legs as if she was going somewhere. Mentally, she was ready to start walking, we just needed to get her stronger.

I came up with an idea I thought would just do the trick. Needing some fabrication, I talked to my father-in-law, Jack, and told him we needed to make Rescue a sling with a hoist so we could put her in the sling and hang her from the beam at the barn. That way, Rescue could touch the ground, bear weight on her legs as she felt like she could and spin herself around to see what was going on. When she got tired, she could just relax and hang. This would allow Rescue to do this at her own pace, to get stronger over time. Soon she would be frolicking in the prairie, just like in my dream. Rescue always had strong willpower, very determined.

Every day Jack had been figuring he'd be digging a hole to bury a goat. But today, instead of digging a hole, he was making a hoist with a sling. And fabricating he did. It was an electric winch with an old tack iron we had laying around the barn. He hooked a towel on the iron and made a perfectly nice sling. Rescue hung like this in the morning and several times throughout the day. She was actually using her front feet to push herself around and turn to see in different directions. It was perfect, a masterpiece in design and function. Rescue liked it, too.

This evening when I went to feed Rescue, her eyes seemed distant. It didn't seem like she would be with us by morning. Even though she enjoyed her new sling, that was not enough. Rescue had been living with confinement for over a week, confined to laying in one spot. She could see and hear the others play but couldn't join them. She relied on us to bring her food and water, to give her attention. Her babies frolicked and played around her, yet she couldn't go with them when they wandered off. She was bedridden – couldn't stand, couldn't roll over. She managed to scoot herself a little, and the effort was all the exercise she got.

Rescue didn't have walls or cages confining her, but she had an illness that confined her to a small space, even though she could see across the fields. She had people and animals loving and caring for her. The dogs even laid next to her for comfort. Yet she was confined. Even so, she always had her head up and ears perked when she heard the gate open or heard our voices. She was in an area where everyone walked by, heavily trafficked so she was never alone, yet her confinement was hers and hers alone to bear. As I left, I told Rescue to send me a dream and I would come stay with her in the middle of the night and hold her so she would not be alone.

It was 4 a.m. that August 4th before I finally fell asleep. I couldn't sleep thinking Rescue was going to let me know she wanted me to come down and sit with her. I had to keep telling myself to go to sleep, she'll let you know. In the morning, I awoke and rushed down to the barn. Knowing that she hadn't sent me a dream, I knew Rescue was either alive and didn't need me or had died and wanted to be alone.

I opened the gate to the barn and there she was, head up high, glad to see me. Once again, I was taken by surprise. I stroked her neck and kissed her nose. I told her how bright-eyed she looked, different from last night. I gave her a bucket of water. I tried to feed her, but she kept turning her head away, pushing her legs around trying to avoid being fed. I kissed her nose and reminded her no one dies of starvation around here, it's the rule! Michael and Jack would hoist her up later for some stretch time.

Rescue died at 4:30 p.m. She was hoisted up on her sling around noon and 3 p.m. Somehow, I think she knew this morning she was near her time and just didn't want to be fussed with. We made sure her babies knew she was gone, although for the last five days they spent much of their time with Sweetie and her babies. Rescue did live the good life here with us. She gave birth to eight kids -- two sets of triplets and one set of twins. Rescue lived with us for four years and four months.

Thank you, Rescue, for the enduring love, passion and strength you showed us. For the messages of "ALL POWER COMES FROM WITHIN" and the reminder to GET ON WITH OUR DREAMS, our journey, and to quit stalling. Thank you for showing us that, even in confinement, we can be strong, we can be loved, and confinement is not just within walls and cages. We must realize confinement can be in many forms and different situations.

*When we look beyond what is directly in front of us,
we are able to open our eyes,
so that we are no longer blinded by the shadow
being cast on and behind us.*
                    by Ahrynn McCann

CHAPTER 11

NEW POSSIBILITIES

It was full-on birthing season. Mama goats and babies were filling the stalls. It was a rainy January 27th, a quiet morning and a perfect time for me to catch up on some much-needed journal entries from the past few days' events. Neither my husband Michael nor I had been down to the barn yet to see if we had any new arrivals.

Around 8:30 a.m., we wandered down to check and found Ruby stuffed in the corner of the large, airy stall. Today it was Ruby's turn, triplets no less, three boys. The stall was crowded with a few llamas, sheep and other goats. We had a hard rain that night and, with all the individual stalls already filled with mamas and babies, it was share or get wet.

It appeared as though they had all agreed to share the one stall. As we made our way past the other animals toward Ruby, we saw that two of the babies were still wet, curled up next to her side. The third baby was laying in front of Ruby, lifeless. The larger, dead boy was twice the others' size and had the full dark-red head all the way to his shoulders. He was perfect in every way. His eyes were closed, his mouth was closed, so it appeared as though he never took a breath. The other two boys were much smaller, white, with light-brown heads and necks.

Surprised that one of Ruby's babies was dead, we looked at each other and tried to figure out what might have happened. Ruby is an experienced mother, with many seasons and several triplets. We considered maybe it was so crowded the baby was laid on or stepped on. Or maybe he was the first one born and, being the biggest, maybe she wasn't dilated enough and he was in the birth canal too long and suffocated. What if we had come down earlier? Would it have been early enough to assist, or was he dead before he was even born? We just didn't know.

We realized Ruby had already accepted that he was dead and she would only have two to raise. I picked up the lifeless body, not yet stiff, and put him in a large bucket. I had received thoughts from the Universe that I was to allow myself to be used as a vessel to energetically scan his body for answers. I questioned whether or not I heard this correctly and received intuitive confirmation that I did. I reminded myself I had taken a two-day hands-on course on how to perform body scans on animals to determine areas of injury or blocked energy. In this class, we learned processes and procedures while working on the instructor's horses, but I didn't know if I was ready for this.

Since my training was on live animals, not animals that had already passed, I questioned whether the theories and practices would still be valid. This was an opportunity to find out. I knew, if for some reason, the outcome was not to my expectations or preconceived ideas, it was not because it isn't possible but that maybe I was not ready or was not properly prepared to allow this experience to take place.

Later that afternoon, the rain had finally stopped and the sun was out to warm the day. A perfect setting to do my work, the body scan, before we proceeded with burial detail. I took the lifeless body to a nice sunny area where we could overlook the foothills and enjoy the warmth. I placed the baby on some hay in the wheel barrel and pulled up a chair so we would both be comfortable. I proceeded to ask for guidance and assistance from the Universe. I stated my plea -- to experience being a vessel to allow energy to flow through me to this baby, scan the body and understand the cause of death.

After centering myself, I closed my eyes and placed my hands on his head and heart, then moved my hands to his hips and across his entire cold body just as I had been trained and asked for guidance. The color I saw was red, and then the red was replaced with white. I also saw two black specks, like the black dots on a die for the number two, spaced just about as far apart. These two black specks moved around in a fluid-like motion. They moved in circles all about the white-colored background. I asked that I would remember the events and opened my eyes to gaze upon him. I opened his eyelid to glance into his lifeless eye.

Even though I know the eyes of an animal are the gateway to the soul and his soul was no longer in this body, I wanted to look through his eyes. They were a cold blue. I opened his mouth then closed it again. I brushed his hair and asked what happened while I moved my hands along his body. Then I closed my eyes again and was just still. I had my hands on his head and shoulders. I could feel his muscles moving as if he was running. I could see his eyes looking around, I could feel his exuberance for life, yet there was no movement in him. It was as if I was experiencing it with him in another place. It was awesome. I saw the red and white colors again, and the black dots. I still did not know the meaning of these colors or the dots.

With the scan complete, I opened my eyes. Still not knowing why he had died, I did not feel discouraged, defeated nor experience a lack of faith. I accepted what happened for what it was and did, in fact, remember the events so I could write them down. I told him I was sorry he did not live, but in time I would know his purpose.

In order to understand this death, I requested the presence of a spirit guide, Serena, who often provides understanding. As always, she was pleased to be summoned to answer my questions and welcomed my presence. Serena knew I had something on my mind to ask, so she got right to the point and requested I state my questions.

My first question was: "Why did he die?" He was the most beautiful of the three, large and strong, why not one of the others? Serena said: *"He chose to be the one, his purpose was to be born dead. He agreed to this. He was here for you to learn, to be able to feel, to see. He was another teaching tool."*

My second question was: "What is the meaning of the red and white colors I saw?" Serena said: *"The Red is grounding, and the animal was grounded with the earth and Universe and then passed over. The White is the light of God, and this was to let you know the animal had passed over."* So he grounded (Red) and passed over (White).

My third question was: "What is the meaning of the two black specks I saw and the reason for moving in a fluid motion?" Serena said: *"The two black dots represented the pupils of your eyes scanning the body. The fluid motion symbolized you analyzing the process and the information you were receiving."*

My fourth question was: "Why did I feel his muscles moving as if he was running and his eyes looking around and feel his emotion of exuberance when there was no life in him?" Serena said: *"He passed over and was experiencing life on the other side. You had merged with him through your connection as a vessel and were able to experience what he was doing on the other side. That is why you could feel his muscles move as if he was running, because he was. That is why you could see eyes looking around, because he was showing you where he was and how happy he was to be there. He knew he had died to be a teacher and you were learning through him."* He was teaching me another way to experience animal energy, opening my eyes to new possibilities – the merging of two separate and distinct energies.

My questions finished, Serena asked if there was anything else. I said no and thanked her for confirming the meaning of this animal's death and why I saw these things.

Serena then added a few comments of her own. She said: *"You are going to be a teacher. You are learning in real life through these experiences. Your wisdom, intuition and passion is growing and it will continue to grow as you continue to learn and allow yourself to be taught."*

Animals recognize that we have lessons to learn, mountains to climb, journeys to follow, and they volunteer to assist in many ways. What unconditional, sacrificial love they offer!

*Open the eyes of your soul,
once you do, never let them close again,
for the eyes are able to see far beyond
the mystery of life itself!*

by Ahrynn McCann

CHAPTER 12
DON'T SEARCH FOR WHAT ISN'T THERE

I rolled over in bed, pulled the covers up over my shoulders and tucked them loosely under my chin. I briefly opened my eyes, looked out the window and caught a glimpse of the beautiful red and orange sunrise filtered between the spaces in the tree leaves. Smiling a bit, I rolled back over and glanced at the clock. Glaring, bold, red numbers stared back at me -- 5:33 a.m.

Wanting to just snuggle in and go back to sleep gave way to thoughts of watching the sun rise. I hadn't done that for awhile. Without too much self-debate, I tossed back the covers, put feet on the floor, dressed in a long T-shirt and rubber clogs. I walked to the library, clutched the child-size barrel chair in my arms and made my way out to the field among the animals.

With my chair facing East, I sat down and watched the sunrise. Not intending to meditate, I just allowed myself to be present and appreciate the beauty of a summer morning. One by one, the animals started to notice my presence. I glanced back, giving them thoughts of love and acknowledging their presence. Suddenly, without warning, my mind heard loud words – OLGA, she's missing!

Olga was one of our goats. I quickly did a head count, surveyed the stock and, sure enough, Olga was missing. My heart skipped a beat or two as I stood up, no longer interested in watching the sunrise. I started searching for Olga. Just the night before, we had heard coyotes howling in the distance. Could Olga have become their victim?

I checked all the stalls, behind the barn, in the corral, all the fields and along the fence lines. Once finished, I started again. I hadn't found her and was getting even more worried, wondering what could have happened, where she could be.

After 45 minutes of searching, I stopped, took a deep breath and just relaxed. Then it dawned on me – OLGA WAS DEAD, she wasn't here. One year ago, Olga died of a heart attack and we buried her in the middle prairie, only a short distance from where I was sitting in my chair watching the sunrise.

Immediately, my anxiety calmed. Then I thought to myself: How could I have forgotten she had died? Then I knew that when I heard the word "Olga" in my mind, it was her, letting me know she was there in spirit to visit with me. Yet, I heard her name and associated it with her missing. This was a most unusual experience.

I acknowledged Olga's presence and asked what she came to say. She said: *"Don't search for what isn't there."* I replied, "What does that mean, what relevance does that have in my life, right now?"

Olga said: *"Two things. You heard my name and immediately thought I was missing and went searching for me. Although this wasn't the purpose of my visit to you, it ended up being a valuable experience. You heard my name loud and clear, that part was accurate, as I was wanting to communicate with you. Your mind, however, created a scene that was purely fabricated. I have been dead for a year, yet you went searching for me. So understand you must be aware that when you hear things, you might make more of it than what it truly is.*

"Secondly, the intent of my visit was to tell you you must be open to possibilities when you are shown or told things. When you hear something, it may not be absolute. Your finite mind might be limiting your perception or you may add your own thoughts or interpretation to it and then be disappointed it didn't work out as told, when in fact, it worked out exactly as told. You had just created a version that didn't exist.

"But before I could tell you this, you actually experienced it right then, first-hand. You heard my name and immediately thought I was missing and actually went searching for me, Searching for Something That Wasn't There. My true

purpose was to communicate with you. How much better could the lesson have been learned than what you experienced? I was wanting to tell you that when something is foretold to you or information given to you, do not go searching for something that isn't there, for parts or pieces that weren't intended."

As Olga finished speaking to me, I realized the magnitude of what I had just experienced. I thanked her for the lesson, picked up my chair and walked back to the house. My husband was still in bed, but awake. He had thought I left for work early and didn't know I was just out watching the sunrise. I told him about looking for Olga. After a few minutes of my story, he interrupted me to say Olga had died and we buried her and he wondered why I was looking for her. I continued my story, telling him I know what he is saying, but when I finish the story, he will understand.

What I think is ironic is I was blinded to something I knew in order to learn a lesson. I experienced the very real emotions that come with searching for something I thought was missing as if it was happening that very moment. I was very present. In reality, I knew Olga was dead and buried, yet my mind was able to forget that, set that reality aside, and allow me to go "searching for something that isn't there."

Olga said *"searching"* for what isn't there, not *"looking"* for what isn't there. Later, I pondered the difference. Searching is deeper than looking. One "searches" for something they have lost with great intent or emotion, yet one "looks" for something without concern. We need to realize in our lives we don't need to search for things that aren't there. Instead, allow the message or situation to just be pure.

Animals continue to communicate with us even after they have passed. If we listen, we can hear them.

*I am Faith. I am Hope. I am Love.
And if I do not fully understand
the true meaning of these gifts now,
I know I will be shown in my life,
when the time is right!
It is at that moment,
I will have no doubt in my mind that without these,
I would not be alive to Live.*

    by Ahrynn McCann

CHAPTER 13
ACCEPT WHATEVER MAY COME

As I sat in my car at the last signal before arriving at my massage, Precious, our sheep, came to mind. I didn't know why, but I took notice of the thought. I was running a little late, so I hurried into the room, changed and quickly laid flat on my stomach on the massage table.

Now that I was here and not hurrying anymore, I finally relaxed. Since Precious had come to mind moments earlier, I thought now would be a good time to spend in meditation. I knew she wasn't feeling well, and I wanted to communicate with her to see if she could tell me what she was feeling, what she needed or what I could do to help.

I started to clear my mind of the day's activities, trying not to think of the phone calls I didn't make, the emails I didn't respond to or the errands I needed to get done on the way back. I took a few deep breaths and tried to relax.

I had a difficult time relaxing into the meditation as the massage was deep and I was distracted. The masseuse was massaging my back, thumbs under my shoulder blades digging deep underneath, then her fingers were pressing at the top of my shoulder blades and the base of my neck. Then the point of her elbow was circling around my shoulder blade, creating that very indiscernible thought of "Does this really feel good? I'm not relaxing, I am tensing more." But somehow I have convinced myself it is for my own good. After all, that's why I am here. Unable to relax enough to meditate, I gave up and waited until "roll-over" time.

Once rolled over onto my back, I was able to relax. The therapist always had candles burning in the room, and I was impressed to look at the candle to my right. It was small, cup-shaped, clear, with little octagon-like windows. One of the windows caught my attention and I could see the glow of the candle inside.

As I looked at the candle, the scepter rays I always see shot straight to my chest. I welcomed the energy and thanked it for being there. I noticed all the other prisms of the candle were not glowing, they had been darkened, only the prism I was looking at was casting light. This seemed unusual, as this type of candle is meant to emanate light from all windows. It was as if I was looking into something with darkness all around except this one window.

As I accepted this energy into my body, I asked my guide, Michaela, to help me communicate with Precious. I asked Michaela if she would show me how to call upon the Healing Goddess Faery to heal Precious. As I awaited some guidance, I continued to look into the window of the candle and think of Precious. I began to see a picture of her in the middle of the brilliance of the candle's light. The scepter rays were still shooting to my chest. I saw the outline of a sheep in the candle's glow, and as I saw the sheep's figure get more and more discernable and actually stand out as a gray cast, I sent Precious healing energy and told Precious I was placing her in this warm place, that the warmth would heal her all over and asked her to accept it. I continued to send healing, all the while thinking of heat. I definitely felt her connect with me.

Then all of a sudden the intensity of the light grew very strong and brilliant and, in a flash, the light was completely snuffed out. The flame had burned out and the candle was dark. My immediate thought was twofold: Precious had died and the snuffing out of the candle was to let me know she had given her last breath; my second thought was the healing had taken place and I no longer needed the candle or the energy. I felt a lightheartedness, a sense of relief which could go with either death or healing; either way, the feeling of sickness or being uncomfortable was gone.

I was anxious to get home. It didn't bother me to think I might find Precious had died. I was okay with that. I know the healing is for the highest and best good of the animal; if it is the will of the Universe and of the animal to be healed, so be it. If not, then another purpose will be revealed.

If I should come home and find her totally healed, what a testament to the experience! If I should come home and find her neither dead nor healed, then what was the experience to tell me? I decided to delay my trip home so I could go by the office and get my computer. I knew I would want to type up the experience I had with the candle and I didn't want to do it the next morning.

I went to my office to pick up my computer. As I sat the computer on the floor, a very tiny spider, tan in color, went racing across the floor, trying desperately to get out of my way. The spider then ran up the wall and across my computer case. I took notice of the spider. When I went into the other room, I noticed a cricket alongside the baseboard. I had never seen a cricket in my office before in the three years I have been there. I knew it wasn't a coincidence, and I knew I would need to follow through to determine the significance of both the spider and the cricket.

I arrived home and, without going into the house or greeting anyone, I went straight down to the barn to check on Precious. The last few nights she had been sleeping out. It had been warm at night so she didn't go into the stall. It was dark, not much moonlight, so I turned on the barn lights. I didn't see her in the field, nor did I see her in the larger stalls with all the goats.

Then I heard my daughter Ahrynn come through the gate. She said, "Have you seen in the stall yet?" I said, "No, I was looking for Precious but hadn't found her yet." Ahrynn said, "She is in the stall and she was dying. I came down to see you because I didn't want you to just find her and not know. Dad and I saw her laying in the field stretched out flat. We couldn't get her to stand up, she didn't have any strength, so we carried her to the barn and put her in a stall."

Ahrynn asked me if I had received her thoughts about it, as she had sent them to me. I told her I got the impression Precious had died at 7:45 p.m. (that's the time it was when the candle was snuffed out). Ahrynn said she had sent me the thoughts around 7 p.m. and asked that I receive the message when it was the right time. My massage started at 6:45 and ended at 7:45. Not just a coincidence.

I unlatched the sliding lock on the stall gate and went inside. I sat next to Precious on the dirt floor covered in wood shavings. She seemed glad to see me. She was a larger-than-normal sheep, with a black face, large head and white, full-wooled body. She stood tall, with long legs, long body and was as lovable as could be. Her eyes were coal black.

Ahrynn was still there standing outside the stall wall looking in. She said, "I sat with her from 6:15-7 p.m. and did some Reiki (a type of hands-on healing energy) with her and was able to calm her breathing, and she looked better than she did earlier. Dad and I gave her a selenium and penicillin shot." With that said, Ahrynn left to go up to the house and go to bed. I decided to stay with Precious. She was in bad shape. You could hear her throat actually filling with fluid as she tried to breathe and then cough it out. She sounded like she was drowning.

At that moment, I recalled the day Precious arrived nearly eight months earlier. Sickened from abuse and malnourishment, she was nearly dead. We loved her, kept her warm and treated her with antibiotics. Within a short time, she was grazing with the others in the green pastures, savoring the sweet grain and rich hay. She had become strong and healthy.

One day I had some women over for an animal communication class, and Precious was our designated cooperating animal. We sat chairs in the birthing stall, a separate stall constructed with new moms in mind. It was fully enclosed, so it kept us out of the winter cold.

We all sat in our chairs in the stall with Precious in the middle of our circle. The instructor helped us understand the lesson, and we all followed along and did our part. One of the things that came out of this session was that Precious communicated she was grateful for our love and assistance, she wanted to have babies of her own, wanted to be here and would do her part to be healthy and strong.

With my recollection over, I returned my focus back to Precious. I stroked her back, sending her love and telling her it was okay to leave, even though she hadn't had babies yet. I reminded her she had enriched our lives and blessed us. Although she had agreed the first day she was here to hang in and give it her all to get strong and healthy, despite her best efforts, she was never able to totally rid herself of the pneumonia she arrived with. We were only able to temper it and make her more comfortable. I asked her to go, to leave us now and fly free, to return to a better place and know that she served her purpose and it was time to move on. I thanked her for the blessings she gave us, said I would always remember her and asked her to return as one of my animal guides to help teach me through my journey and purpose, to aide in the healing of other animals and in understanding the animal world as a whole. I told her with one passing comes another life. In her death, we would move on together; her in embarking on her next journey and me having shared this journey with her and knowing I can call upon her.

I stayed with Precious for quite awhile. I held her head in my arms so she would be comfortable and waited to see if she was willing to go. This wasn't the first time she had been down, but I thought it was her last time. Then I thought she may surprise us and decide to stick around awhile longer. I wanted to stay with her all night if necessary to keep her company and let her know she wasn't all alone, but I said my goodbyes and thanked her again. If she chooses to stay, this, too, will be a blessing.

As I walked back to the house, I knew the answer to my three possibilities: If in the morning she was dead, the snuffing of the candle was her last breath; if she was alive, the snuffing of the candle meant healing had taken place; if she was neither dead nor healed, what was the experience to tell me... that she chose to wait to die so I could spend the needed time with her. The snuffing of the candle was to impress upon me that matters had been decided and WHAT WILL BE, WILL BE. I had done what I could, all things had been considered, and the plan was unfolding because that is what was to be.

The intensity of the experience, the brilliance of the light, the connection I felt with her, the picture of the sheep in the light is an experience I needed to have. It was to let me know I can communicate and, through this communication, I knew that things were serious, I must take action and pay attention, not just pass it off as it couldn't be or it really wasn't a sign of something real.

I almost didn't want to wake in the morning. The thought of going down to the barn, not knowing if Precious had struggled and fought to stay alive only to have given into death or if, in fact, she was alive and well and had accepted the healing and wants to be here a while longer. Whatever her choice, I was ready to accept.

First thing when I woke up I thought of Precious. I didn't waste time getting properly dressed. Instead, I put on a robe, slipped on shoes and went to the barn. I anticipated finding Precious dead, and I was right. She looked peaceful. I know I helped calm her, made her not feel so alone, and I looked forward to hearing her spirit on my walks.

My answer: The snuffing of the candle meant she chose to wait to die so I could be with her, but matters had been decided and what is, was. Even though Precious had died, my experience didn't end with her death. I had yet to discover the meaning of the cricket and the spider I just happened to notice at the office.

CRICKET:
The cricket is associated with intuition and belief. Some crickets can't fly and are therefore grounded. For me, the cricket had significance in bringing the awareness I needed to be grounded and balanced. Because crickets are night creatures, they must effectively use what light is available and trust their intuition in the dark. This, too, was significant for me. I needed to believe and trust in what I was feeling with Precious, the messages I was receiving from the animals.

SPIDER:
Spiders are designers and weavers. They design their webs so the threads going around the circle are sticky and the threads going from the center to the outside edge are not sticky. If we are going in circles, we will get stuck; if we go direct, we are free. As weavers, the spiders are telling us our past influences our future. What we weave now will affect our future. What we think, how we feel, what we do is weaving a pattern. Spiders spin their webs and then wait; they do their work and wait. If we do our work, results will come.

I didn't have any reference books in my personal library that provided information on animals and what they mean spiritually. I remembered a book I had seen in certain practitioner's library called "*Animal Speak*" by Ted Andrews. In my quest to finish this experience, I ventured to the bookstore. The first bookstore was out. The second bookstore, the same thing, out. However, this store had another book by the same author titled "*Animal Wise.*" With my purchase in hand, I was anxious to read and learn.

I think it quite amazing how the Universe provided both a cricket and a spider that night. In looking at the two, it is evident I was being brought a message of trusting my intuition, the power of belief, to stay balanced and grounded while listening to my intuition, to welcome and accept the possibilities of new beliefs and paths in my life, to be direct, to set my intentions for my new path and the Universe will provide the experience, and the results will come, to trust what I feel, not what I see, and that healing energies are being awakened within me. (It is five days later, and I haven't seen the cricket or the spider in my office again.)

*Embrace the unknowns of your heart,
that moment of time when everything seems to be out of control
or unfit in our lives.
For it is the unknowns, that truly teach us
how to Embrace those next moments
life will give us once again.*

by Ahrynn McCann

CHAPTER 14

LIFE IS UNCERTAIN
Make It Wonderful!

It was a typical October morning, cool breeze, the sun shining, leaves on the trees turning autumn colors. You could smell the change in season. The animals were getting their winter coats and sleeping in the barns at night, a reminder that it wouldn't be too long before the rains would come and the ground would be muddy. But until then, the animals were out enjoying the sun, some grazing, some eating the fresh feed in the feeders, others stretched out on the prairie grass basking in the sun.

In the stillness of the morning, a sharp, clear gun-shot was heard. Living in the country, you expect that now and then, but this seemed out of place, random. It wasn't until later that we realized the impact that shot really had on our lives and others in our rural community.

The local paper called us from the information retrieved from the report we had filed with the local sheriff's office. The reporter wanted to do an interview. Rather than provide a telephone interview, I offered to write my story and send it to him, with instructions that he could reprint it word-for-word or use parts of it.

My Official Registered Name is RUNNING BEAR, but I was often called "RB"; I didn't mind.

My original owner died and the ranch was too much for his wife to take care of. Her daughter drove by another ranch every day on her way to work and noticed how well-cared-for all the animals were. Thinking this would be a perfect place for me to live, she stopped and asked the owners of the ranch if they would take me in. She told them I was a "guard llama."

In case you didn't know, we all have different jobs. Some llamas are for show, to walk a certain way and win trophies and ribbons. Others are raised for the wool, and still others are used for packing in the wilderness. I was a guard llama. I was responsible for the sheep. Every day I led the sheep out to pasture to graze in the fields and protected them from predators. At evening time, it was my job to make sure they were safely back in the barn and guard them at night from predators, too. I enjoyed my job. My record was impeccable; I never lost a sheep.

My new owners had never had a guard llama. They had packing llamas and a couple that were just good ol' pets. They weren't sure how I would fit in, but they were willing to give it a try. They promised my current owner that if I didn't work into the herd or adjust, they would be sure to find me a good home.

Sybil, Kalysta, RB

It wasn't long before my new owners arrived to take me away. They could tell I wasn't too sure about leaving my sheep. After all, they were my responsibility.

My new home was fantastic. Lots of other animals were around, including llamas. I had been the only llama at my other home, so this was going to be different.

Since I didn't have my sheep, my new owners put goats in the pasture. They knew it would be easier for me to adjust if I had animals to herd and could do my job. I found that goats are different than sheep. They don't pack tightly together and don't like to be herded out so early in the morning. They are more lazy than the sheep. At night they don't like to go to the barn, they want to sleep out in the field and graze all night. So I slept out in the field with them, to protect them. That was my job, to guard. I missed my sheep!

My owners could tell this arrangement just wasn't working. They made another trip back to my old house, loaded my sheep and brought them to join me in the pasture. It was just like old times, just me and my sheep!

I made sure to take my sheep out to pasture and back to the barn every day. After a few months, I began to spend more time at the fence with the other llamas and less time with my sheep. I became more comfortable with my new home and fit in.

RB

I enjoyed my new home very much. I had the run of several acres, tall and roomy barns, water misters in the summer for us to keep cool, fresh hay and grain on a regular basis. We received a lot of attention, too. My owners brought us fresh leaves from the trees in the summer and fall, almonds and peaches from the trees in the backyard and, of course, all the trimming's from the household fruit (cantaloupe rinds, grapes, bananas, strawberry tops and anything else that didn't need to go to waste). We were all spoiled, and we loved it!

The vet came twice a year to trim our feet, give us shots and a general look-over. I didn't really care for the pasty stuff that went in my mouth, but the others took it, and so did I. All in all, it wasn't too bad (for my "best good," they said).

I watched as some animals departed from our home. You see, my owners had a "refuge ranch." They took in animals that had been abused or left for dead and nursed them back to health. The animals stayed on the ranch to live out the rest of their lives, however long that might be, to live in comfort, never abused or mistreated. They also had babies from the mama goats every year. That was a fun time, lots of little ones running around. They took extra care of the sick ones, taking turns at night coming down to the barn to feed or care for them. They were usually with them when they died, didn't want anyone to be alone. We all had automatic water and heat lamps in the winter to keep warm, fresh straw for comfort and, of course, we got brushed and fussed with, too.

However, all this ended for me on Thursday, October 25. I had just finished eating the morning hay and decided to take in some sun on this fine fall day. I was laying on the hillside near the fence at the road. I didn't mind the sound of the cars passing by. Then, all of a sudden, I felt something strange pierce my side. I began to gasp for air. I didn't know what was wrong, but something definitely wasn't right. I was in so much pain. Even though I had never experienced this before, I knew it wasn't right. I fell on my side, thrashed around, trying in every way to get back up. Then it happened, my last breath, I was gone.

My owners were home earlier in the morning and heard a shot but, being out in the country, they hear that every now and then. It wasn't until they were on their way back home from town that they noticed I was laying downhill and motionless. They came over to see me and found me lifeless, no breath. They noticed I had thrashed my head and legs from side to side in an attempt to right myself on the hillside. There was a pool of blood around my head.

Even though my owners could not find a bullet wound, they figured I must have been shot, and the sound they heard earlier was not just someone shooting a target, it was my life being extinguished. They took good care of me in death, just as they did in life. They took me to Davis for a complete autopsy to verify cause of death. The report stated I was indeed shot. The bullet entered along my side between my ribs, then through the left lung, through the esophagus, through the right lung and into my thoracic vertebrae. I drowned in my own blood. My lungs and esophagus filled with blood instead of air, and I suffocated to death. It was not a quick death, I suffered a lot of pain and discomfort. No one was there to hold me and comfort me at my death. I was in perfect health, just taking in some morning sun, when my life, in an instant, was taken from me.

My life was cut short and I was not ready to leave this wonderful home. I had a good life and lived it well. I hope my death will not go unnoticed. What they did was cruel, I SUFFERED!! My owners do everything they can to give animals a second chance at life through their dedication and willingness to sacrifice for the animals on this ranch. Yet someone decided to take a perfectly healthy life without a second thought.

That was what I wrote to the reporter as if the animal was telling the story. The paper never published the story in full or in part. The reporter's comments were that "…the format of having the llama speaking in written word was too awkward for me to use in the final story." So he was "unable to use the material."

I hadn't intended for this story to be a chapter in this book, but one day, months after the incident, I heard RB's voice. Not really having communicated with him much while he was alive, I was surprised. He said he wanted to tell the story his own way. After hearing his version, I retrieved the story I had written to the newspaper and added RB's version to it. He had communicated to me, and I believed it was important. Here is the story as told by RB.

My owner wrote a story on my behalf for the newspaper after the incident. She did a fine job, I must say, but I would like to tell the parts she couldn't.

I was born across the way from my original owners. I didn't travel far when I left my birthplace to go to my first home. It was an easy adjustment. I didn't know I was a guard llama, I guess it was just natural for me. I didn't receive special training to guard, I just did it.

I was always the only llama at my home. Guarding my sheep was all I knew. My owner would come out to see us, and he always had grain in his shirt pocket for me. It was his way of getting me to come close.

I don't know why I was always reserved and didn't want attention. I was more the observer. Maybe that's part of being a guard llama, always watching and observing. That didn't change when I came to the new ranch. When I arrived, I was amazed at all the other animals. I had always been the only llama and here there were three others and many more sheep and goats than I was used to. I was relieved when they kept me separate from the others. All I had to do was guard my sheep. I eventually settled in and got used to the idea of having a bigger family. Besides, most of the sheep knew what to do anyway, so my job was pretty easy.

But one thing didn't change; just like at my other home, I always kept my distance. I watched my new owner brush and fuss over the others. They respected that I didn't want to be fussed over but always offered, just the same. In the months before I died, I started letting them get closer. They actually brushed me head-to-tail, side-to-side, and I did like it. They were glad I let them. Jack (the llama in charge of us) was a little put out, as he never had to share attention with me before. I even started coming closer when they offered me treats, and I would let them pet me as they walked by. It wasn't so bad, just different.

I remember the time my owner took us out to the lake. She took me and Jack. She had a difficult time loading me in the trailer at home, tried everything and, once I finally went in, wondered how she was going to get me back in the trailer at the lake to come home. We went for a nice walk around the point. Jack was anxious the entire walk; he wanted to get back home to be with Georgette (his llama girlfriend). I didn't mind the walk; it was nice to go somewhere.

Sometimes we like to see a different place, do different things, just like you. We don't get bored, as you say you do, for we are very present beings, no past or future, just now. But a change is nice now and then. It gives us different smells and sights and appreciation.

On the way back, my owner was wondering how she was going to get me loaded. She knew how difficult it was at home, and now she had to do it again without as many people to help. My owner decided to ask Jack to tell me to load. She and Jack had talked before. Jack told me to just step up and walk right in, we were only going home, no big deal. He told me our owner asked him to do this. We got to the trailer, she opened the door and swung it wide, and Jack went in first as a way of showing me how it's done, then it was my turn. My owner took my lead rope, walked me up to the back and up I stepped and in I went, just like a professional. She smiled and was pleased with my performance. She thanked me for the easy load. When we got home and unloaded, she thanked Jack for talking to me and getting me to load. Then to her surprise, she heard me say, "The next time you want me to do something, you should ask me directly, not ask Jack to ask me." That was a special moment for both us, since we had not communicated before. She thanked me and said she would do that in the future.

Most of the animals in this book knew they were dying and, at such time, provided lessons/experiences for others. My story is about death and dying, but not one we shared. Neither of us knew I was going to die that day. We didn't have time to spend together. I died alone. Although other animals were around, I was alone. My death was sudden. I didn't have a disease that took time to kill me. I didn't get sick enough to die. Yet, the time it took for me to die did not seem quick. I was in pain. I did not know what happened. I did not have anyone there to help me let go, as you did with many others.

I guess my message would be that LIFE IS UNCERTAIN. We might just get too comfortable, thinking things are always the way they are. In my case, I ate hay, grazed the green grass, walked from one prairie to another, very content knowing all was in order, no worries of any threats or changes. Then, in an instant, it all changed, life was being taken, no time for goodbyes or questions or asking if things can be different.

I really don't know how to describe my death other than panic and uncertainty, not knowing why I was feeling the way I was. I can describe my life: WONDERFUL! I had it all, love, compassion, freedom, importance. I was strong, healthy, happy.

LIFE IS UNCERTAIN. Everyday confirm that LIFE IS WONDERFUL. We do not know when it might end. I know if you had been at my side when I died, I would have been comforted. I know you wouldn't have been able to save my life, but dying would have been more comfortable.

Each and every one of the animals' stories are different about life and death. I guess my story is about Surprises. Be certain you are happy and that life is wonderful; there may not be another day to change it. Right what isn't. Have no regrets. Make today be worth something; it might be all you have.

As a continuing testimony to RB that his death, and the deaths of the other animals at the hands of the shooters that same day, did not go unnoticed, the alleged shooters were apprehended. Both were 18 years old and were charged with cruelty to animals, negligent discharge of a firearm, shooting from a public roadway and shooting from a vehicle. One shooter was initially sentenced to a maximum of one year in the County Jail, and the other shooter to a maximum of eight years and four months in federal prison. According to the reports filed, confirmed deaths included two goats, two dogs, one bull, one chicken and one llama (RB). One dog and one goat survived their injuries. There may have been more deaths or injuries, but that is all that was officially reported by the owners of the animals who perished that day.

*Listen, Feel and Embrace the wisdom
and guidance of the Universe,
the Colors of the most beautiful sunrises to sunsets,
the wind and rain and sun of Mother Nature,
the water beneath the mountain terrain
and the valleys of grass lands that can be seen
as far as our eyes will lead.
All the beauty in all of the world
and we are able to see it all
in the blink of an eye!*

by Ahrynn McCann

CHAPTER 15
REGINALD: THE LAST CHAPTER

My daughter Ahrynn and I walked out of the automatic doors at the local veterinary clinic, arms around each other, tears still falling from our eyes as we consoled each other. I thanked her for being there for Reggie and I knew it was hard. She said, "Mommy, when I was in the room with Monkey (this is Ahrynn's special name for Reggie) just a little while ago, you know what he said to me? He said he was the last chapter in your book and he was going to help you finish it." That made me cry all the more.

This emotional event started just a couple days earlier. Ahrynn had been moved to Oregon for six weeks and decided to visit us for a week. Michael and I had plans to be gone to Arizona for ten days. The day before we left, we had played with all three dogs out in the prairie, a typical day of play in good weather. We would kick the ball, and Reggie, the Jack Russell, would hurry to get the ball first, while the dalmation, Kylle, was chasing at his heels. Even though the dalmation could easily overpower the Jack Russell, it was truly a game between the two of them -- one likes to chase, the other to be chased. The Lab, Two-Bitts, didn't care much for the game, so he would just go off on his own and dig for gophers. When the other two are through playing, he returns.

Expecting it to be a typical trip as before, we loaded the car, said our goodbyes to all the animals and started the 10½ hour drive to Arizona. We arrived on Sunday, as usual, exhausted from the trip. The next morning, we were out and about town when we received a phone call from Ahrynn. She was very hysterical and we knew immediately something was wrong. She was crying into the phone and said Monkey was hurt really, really bad. He was running to get the ball and he just started crying and couldn't move his back end at all, he was in so much pain. We didn't stay on the phone long, as Ahrynn needed to immediately tend to Reggie. I tried to calm her over the telephone, telling her to take deep breaths. It was hard to be strong and not get hysterical myself, but every minute could make a difference to Reggie.

I hung up with Ahrynn and called Michael's parents to pick her and Reggie up and then called the vet to advise of an emergency admit. Then we just waited. It wasn't too much later that we received the return call we knew would change our day, our plans and, most likely, our lives. "Mommy," Ahrynn said, "it doesn't look good. We have two choices. Surgery or steroids. If you do surgery, it has to be now and he has to go to another clinic. They can't do the surgery here. If you do the steroids, he has to stay here overnight. The x-rays show his spinal cord is being compromised in several places, but they can't tell the extent of compromise without a neuropathy, which injects a dye into the spinal cord to see how restricted it is. That's all I know. Do you want to talk to the doctor?" I said yes, have the doctor call us right back so we can ask more questions.

A few seconds later, we were speaking to the doctor. She wasn't able to tell us much more than Ahrynn did, other than the difference between the surgery and steroids. She explained he had arthritis in the lower part of his back/hips from an obvious prior injury and that there appeared to be several other areas along his spine that showed trauma or weakness as well. Although he had lost mobility and control of his lower body, the major focal point of this injury appeared to be more in the upper spine.

I told the doctor he was a very active dog, very physical and very strong. I inquired as to whether or not the surgery would be something that might need to be repeated later. If his spine appears to be weakened, are we just setting him up for more surgeries? The doctor explained that, yes, it is possible he could re-injure another part of his spine down the road.

She explained the other option for treatment was steroids which, if successful, could mean he would regain most, if not all, of his mobility and be just as active as before. The only issue was, if we did not opt to do surgery now, as time goes by the benefits of the surgery decrease significantly. The steroids have to be administered for 24 hours in order to know if they will work.

The doctor knew she needed to give us some words of encouragement, so she added that the positive for Reggie is, even though he didn't have mobility in the lower half of his body, he did pull his leg back when she touched his foot. She had treated other animals with worse symptoms that responded positively to steroid treatments. Michael and I discussed the options and decided to go with the steroids. It seemed as though the surgery option was putting him through too much based on the severity and having to worry about limiting his play later. It would be so difficult for him to not be active.

We wouldn't know anything more until the next day. The doctor said if he had improved by morning, she would be able to send him home with oral steroids and pain medication. He would have to be kept still in a crate for two weeks for healing. If he was worse, surgery would not be an option and more steroids would not make a difference.

The rest of the day we were just sick to our stomachs. Nothing else mattered. All we could do was hope that, because he had some neurological response to her touching his foot, it was a good sign that he would get better on the steroids.

As Michael and I tried to sort our feelings and plan for the decisions we might have to make, I told him if the steroids didn't work, I would like to take Reggie home and work with him. I knew it would take a lot of dedication, but I would do Reiki hands-on healing, massage his body, and take him to our friend for some alternative natural-healing procedures. I told Michael when we as humans are struck with an injury without warning and end up in the hospital on life support, we don't just pull the plug, we try every option possible, and I felt the same way about Reggie. Many people sacrifice something to help another person, we are no different with our animals.

We had only been in Arizona for one day when that phone call changed our plans. We kept replaying the conversations and discussing the same things over and over. We couldn't do anything, didn't enjoy eating or going places. We couldn't sleep that night, so we packed up and, at 3 a.m., began the long journey back home to see Reggie. Another 10 ½ hour drive, and the doctor would be calling us around 9:30 or 10 a.m. to let us know what his condition was.

The ride was quiet at times, as both of us were reliving our joys with Reggie, the things that made him so special. Then one of us would bring up a subject to distract us from those thoughts. We knew each of us was hurting in our own way. Even though Reggie was Michael's dog, he was close to the entire family, as all our pets are. As the clock neared 9 a.m., we both just stared out the car windows. We knew we would be hearing soon. Even though we were optimistic, it was that moment of uncertainty that created such silence.

Around 10 a.m. the phone rang. I was driving, so Michael took the call. It was the doctor and, unfortunately, Reggie was worse. The steroids didn't work and, at this point, surgery was not an option. She said not only did the steroids not work, but they couldn't keep his pain managed, and he was in a lot of pain. Her suggestion was to put him down. She knew we were in Arizona, but did not know we had already left for home. We told her we were only four hours from the clinic and to wait for us to arrive.

We called Ahrynn to let her know what Reggie's condition was and that we would call her when we were about 30 minutes out so she could meet us at the clinic. Although the doctor felt the best option now was to put Reggie down, she did not know of our plans to bring him home and do alternative therapies. We called Michael's parents to let them know we would be there soon to see Reggie and would let them know what happens. Reggie was a big part of their life, too. When we are gone, he would often stay at our house by day to play with the dogs and go to their house for a "sleep over" at night. He had his own bed, toys, leash and everything at their place. They went for walks and he played at the creek, chased squirrels and cats. He loved going for "sleep overs" at Grandma's.

After hearing the news, I called our chiropractic friend to see if he could meet us that afternoon to assess Reggie and begin treatments. He said the important thing to consider is whether or not he had control of his bowels. He said he was available and to call him as soon as we had Reggie and he could meet us.

The rest of the ride was even more quiet. Even though we had made up our minds to take Reggie home, what if things changed when we got there, what if we have to put him down? We weren't prepared for that. We both had tears of our own as we drove the remaining miles home. Our backs were aching from the strain of driving and the emotions we were feeling. Neither of us had any appetite. Neither of us recalled the scenery of the roads traveled, the towns we passed through or the rest stops we visited. We were in a hypnotic state, hypnotized by our own fear, our love and the shock of the prior 24 hours.

While we were traveling, my phone rang. It was Michael's mom. She said Ahrynn had told her of our plans to take Reggie home and do alternative healing therapies. She said she decided to ask the spirit guides for direction, and the guide said to let Reggie go, this is best for him. She was in tears telling me this, as she knew as well as I did this meant Reggie would have to be put to sleep and we would not have him around to bring us joy and laughter. I thanked her for sharing this with us and I would remember it when we see Reggie. I told Michael about the phone call. Hanging on to the hope that we could somehow keep him, I told him we would wait to decide until we saw Reggie and I was still willing to dedicate the time and energy to his healing and recovery.

A few miles from the clinic, we stopped at the store to purchase a "jimmy." This is what we called Reggie's favorite toy. It was just a stuffed animal that had a squeaker in it. Every time we came home from the store with plastic grocery sacks, he just knew there was a jimmy in it for him. Stopping for the toy was yet another emotional time, as we knew this was like taking flowers to a loved one in the hospital. It was hard knowing this might be his last jimmy. The store didn't have the typical squeaker toy, so Michael got the closest thing he could with a squeaker.

We drove into the parking lot at the vet and Ahrynn was already there waiting. She got out of the truck, and in her hands was the jimmy Reggie had last been playing with. I gave her a hug and told her thanks for thinking to bring it, and we showed her the one we had just purchased. Walking through the automatic doors into the building, smelling the clinical sterile air, walking up to the front desk and asking to see Reggie was heart-wrenching. Knowing we were finally going to see him, be able to offer comfort and love and that he would have family by his side was comforting after the long drive, but we also knew we would see him in pain.

The three of us waited in the exam room while they went to get Reggie for us. After a very long drive, we were finally going to see him. As they brought him through the door, you could see the pain in his face. His eyes were glassy, his hips were drawn up, he was tense in his face, with wrinkles around his nose. He actually looked like a different dog. We had never seen him in so much pain.

When he heard our voices you could tell he recognized them, but he was on such high doses of pain medication, he couldn't quite respond like he wanted to. Emotions escalating, the three of us immediately teared up. The assistant set Reggie down on the table on a blanket. Michael put his arms around him, Ahrynn and I just stayed close. I noticed Reggie calm down. He had been shaking fervently when he was first brought in, but in Michael's arms he regained calmness, a sense of love and unity. He knew his family was with him, yet he still had emptiness in his eyes.

Michael gave him the new squeaky toy, squeezed it so it would make the sound. Reggie heard the familiar sound and perked up his ears, lifted his head and acted as if he was ready to play. Ahrynn showed him his other jimmy, soft and cuddly. He rubbed his head on it with the other toy in his mouth. For a moment I thought this was proof he could deal with the pain, as long as he was with us and had his toys, he could manage. But a few seconds later, his brightness left and he returned to showing signs of pain. At least for a few moments, we were able to distract him from his pain and give him joy.

After Michael spent some time with Reggie, Ahrynn and I gave him our love, too. I put my hands on him and did some Reiki. I told him we loved him, thanked him for being such a joy to us. We knew after seeing him like this, there was only one option, to put him to sleep. We called our son Joshua at work to let him know so he could come to the clinic right away to say his goodbyes.

While we waited for Joshua to arrive, we asked questions of the doctor. We explained about our unwillingness to give up too easily, that both of us were available for 24-hour care and treatments. What about the option of a cart so he could still get around and play and enjoy life to the fullest? She could see we were willing to explore all options but reminded us they could not keep his pain managed. He was being given the highest level of pain medicine (equivalent to morphine for us) and still experiencing pain, and she believed it was asking too much of him to endure. She said he is a wonderful dog. Despite the level of pain, he never tried to bite them, allowed them to examine and care for him; he knew they were trying to help, but despite all of this and his apparent willingness to cooperate, she felt euthanasia was the only option. She was in favor of alternative therapies, even carts, if he could manage the pain. Then she said he did not have control of his bowels and that they had to extract urine via a catheter, as he could not do this on his own. Remembering what our friend had said about his bowels and recalling what the guide had said about letting Reggie go and seeing the pain he was in, we agreed to the euthanasia.

By this time, Joshua had arrived and joined us in the exam room. Now the four of us comforted Reggie. Michael and I left the room to allow the two children time to be alone with Reggie. We went into another empty exam room and held each other and made sure we both felt we were doing the right thing. Michael said when Reggie goes, he wanted me to be the one holding him. He said, "You have a gift, and I want to be sure Reggie leaves us peacefully, without a fight, and I want you to do that for him."

Although it was so difficult, we signed the consent form for the euthanasia and returned to the room where Reggie was. We asked the children if they were ready, if they had enough time, and they said yes. Before the doctor came in, I spent a few minutes with Reggie. I mentally showed him what was going to happen, he was going to go to sleep, he would be free of pain and Pepper (the German shorthair that passed earlier) would be there to see him. I thanked him for being such a joy in our lives and that, although we would miss him, this was best. I told him he could still join us at the swing as Pepper does and Kylle would still be "watching for him."

As I told him all of this, I was doing Reiki on him, and I felt the peace come over his body. He lifted his head and stared into my eyes. As I looked into his eyes, I saw deep into his soul and he thanked me, we connected on a soul level, and I knew all would be well. Through his eyes, he said goodbye.

Although it is emotional connecting with an animal through their eyes, it is true through their eyes we see the animal's soul, and what a gift Reggie gave me in his last few minutes of life! The doctor entered the very silent room and made sure we were all ready. Michael told the doctor I had to hold Reggie while she administered the injection. I held him, sent him Reiki and told him it was okay to go, to release his soul from this painful body and meet Pepper and live, be happy, it was okay.

We watched him close his eyes and relax, he was gone. More tears, yet joy that he was released from his pain. There was sadness, too, because the accident happened so suddenly, without warning. Opting to take Reggie home to bury him, Michael picked him up in a towel, cuddled him in his arms and took him out to the car while I stayed behind to take care of the final paperwork and charges. Ahrynn waited with me. Arms around each other, tears still falling from our eyes, we walked out the automatic doors and Ahrynn said, "Mommy, you know what Monkey said to me? He said he was the last chapter in your book and that he was going to help you finish it." I cried all the more.

The four of us went home to bury Reggie. Michael held him in his lap while I drove. What a whirlwind few days this had been! We had physical exhaustion from driving, emotional exhaustion and yet the final step had to occur, burial. We still had one important event to get through, making sure the other two dogs knew Reggie was gone. We believe the animals grieve and need time to release and have peace, too.

Ahrynn had put Kylle and Two-Bitts in the laundry room when she left to come to the clinic. With Reggie in my arms, I opened the doggie gate to the laundry room, laid Reggie on the floor in front of the dogs and told them that their buddy and friend was gone. As Reggie lay lifeless on the floor, neither of the dogs wanted to get close. The black Lab, Two-Bitts, who was laying on the floor, sniffed from a distance, rolled up his nose and scooted his body 180 degrees away from Reggie, toward Michael, and his entire body shook as he cried. He was literally moaning and crying while shaking, not just a little shake like he was cold or nervous, rather an entire body shake, he was grieving.

Kylle reacted differently. Kylle and Reggie were close. Just like many relationships, they loved each other and hated each other. Kylle was the chaser, Reggie was the chased. Kylle was standing. He kept turning and walking away, then he would come back a little closer and then turn away again, like he didn't want to know. It was too hard to see his best buddy lifeless. Finally, Kylle came close enough to sniff. Two-Bitts had turned himself back around, and Kylle went over to Two-Bitts and the two of them licked each other's faces as if to share in the loss, the grief, and console each other.

We opened the door to go outside. Michael went to get the tractor so he could dig a hole, and I took the three dogs to the swing. The swing is our quiet place, our place to just sit and be still, to be together. When Pepper was alive, it was understood by all that I sat in the middle, with Two-Bitts on my left, Pepper on my right, while Kylle sat at the tree and "watched" to be sure the little dog, Reggie, did not come into our space. It was Kylle's job to watch so we could have our time together.

This was a space where Reggie was not permitted. As we would sit on the swing, we would see Reggie out in the distance, and Kylle would be there growling and barking at him, assuring him he was close enough. Kylle had a job to do and he did it well. Kylle did not sit on the swing with us. Just Pepper, Two-Bitts and me.

Then, when Pepper died, there was an empty spot on the swing. Kylle decided he still had a job to do, so he didn't fill the empty spot, it was just Two-Bitts and me on the swing. Kylle still watched. He still did his job of keeping the little dog far enough away so we could have our special time. Oh, Kylle would leave his post and jump on the swing in Pepper's spot, but only for a moment, then he would be down again and off to his post. He just wanted to be sure I knew he was doing his job, and I did.

The day of Reggie's burial was different. I sat in the middle with Reggie's lifeless body in my lap, Two-Bitts sat on the left and Kylle sat on the right, in Pepper's spot. He knew there was no reason to watch at his post anymore, there wasn't a little dog to keep at a distance, there wasn't any special time to protect anymore. The interesting thing about this is that Kylle sat up straight in the swing and WATCHED intently as Michael brought the tractor around. He WATCHED him leave the shop area, go through the gate to the street. He WATCHED him drive down the street to the next gate. He WATCHED him open the gate and come into the backyard. He never took his eyes off of Michael, as if he knew the tractor was going to bury Reggie and he wanted to be sure it was coming. He had a glare and a stare to his watch.

Michael decided where to put the grave, dug the hole and came over to get Reggie from my arms. He thought the dogs should go inside so they wouldn't dig up the grave later. I told him it would be fine, they needed to be there.

We put Reggie in the grave and rounded up all his toys, all his "jimmies," including the one we had just bought him. We placed a new tree on top of his grave, an evergreen bottlebrush. We walk by it everyday. That's what Michael wanted, a tree planted somewhere visible and evergreen to symbolize that Reggie lives on in our hearts. We gave each other a hug. I told Ahrynn I was sorry she had to experience the accident and take care of Reggie in such pain, but we were glad she was home when it happened so he wasn't alone.

We all knew the next few days or even weeks would be difficult, tears shed over the little things that are just always there. Reggie wouldn't be there to greet us at the gate upon coming home, he wouldn't be there to tuck us into bed with his goodnight snoodles, he wouldn't be there to race from one end of the property to the other to beat us, he wouldn't be there for that trip to town for a treat and to smell our fingers to make sure we shared it with him.

I had tears in my eyes going to bed that first night, knowing Reggie wouldn't be snuggling in with us or laying next to the bed to sleep. I was emotionally drained, yet found it difficult to drift off to sleep. I guess once I finally did go to sleep it was a deep sleep, because the next thing I knew, I was awakened by Reggie's bark. It was a loud, crisp, happy bark, no mistaking it for anything else. I knew he had made the trip, he was happy, pain-free and was letting me know all was well.

The next day, Wednesday, was the day Ahrynn was suppose to return to

Oregon. She decided she needed to stay one more day and would leave Thursday morning. Her church was having an Ash Wednesday celebration, so she decided to go. That night, she asked me if I would sleep with her, so I did.

As we laid in bed, she said, "Mommy, you know what Monkey said to me at church tonight? He said if you get a ball and leave it in the house, you will know he had been visiting when you see it moved." Once again, tears welled in my eyes. I knew what that was about. His energy will be with us, and this is his way of making sure we know it is. We had put all the balls and toys in his grave, so we didn't have a ball to leave. It wasn't until the next day when I spoke with Michael's mom that she said they had Reggie's name tag, bed, leash and a squeaky ball. She wanted to know if I wanted any of them. I told her yes, of course. A squeaky ball, how perfect!

As the days and weeks go by, we heal, we do not tear up as much. But we must remember, all life is ENERGY and, as life passes on, we are only discarding the physical body, the energy remains. There's always doubt when things happen so suddenly, no time for thought or preparation. Did we consider all possibilities, were we being selfish? We question ourselves: Did Reggie mean he would be my last chapter in such a way that I was to work with him, do the alternative therapies, allow him to heal and provide us with lessons and stories of encouragement and strength to better help others? Did I cut Reggie short of this by accepting that he was in too much pain? Was it too much? If he was able to be such a good patient and able to play even for brief moments, were we too quick to end his suffering? Is it suffering to them? Only time will tell, as Reggie tells the last chapter. I'm sure he will enlighten us and all these questions will be answered, and in my confusion and second-guessing I will finally know why. One thing we do know is Reggie will be with us, he is pure ENERGY.

It had been two months since Reginald died. I had traveled to Arizona to spend some alone time, quiet my mind, work on myself, reconnect, do some energy work and, of course, I brought the manuscripts with me to work on. I had just finished proofing Reggie's "last chapter" when I sensed his energy around me and I thought he might be letting me know this was the perfect time for us to finish his chapter.

I wasn't sure if the energy I felt was just because of heightened emotions from having just finished reading a very difficult story or if it truly was Reggie's presence. So I went to the closet, grabbed a folding chair, tore off a stack of paper towels for the tears, got a bottle of water, sunglasses, pad/pen and off I went to the sandy beach at the river's edge to allow Reggie to finish The Last Chapter.

With a quiet mind and a willing heart, I asked Reggie to join me. I felt the energy confirmation throughout my body, as I always get when I am "tuned-in." I received direct confirmation from Reggie that he was there. My eyes were closed, and I heard a bird squawk as it flew quickly beside me. I heard Reggie say, *"Remember the blackbirds."* I knew it was him! When I opened my eyes, two blackbirds were perched above me on the rail. Here is Reggie's message:

"My story is not unusual. What happened to me is not uncommon. Running and frolicking, innocent play and enjoyment suddenly changed. I had been experiencing discomfort for awhile. Remember how I would wait for you to sit down in your room and would curl up beside your feet for your famous spinal rub? Remember how I always stretched out when you got to my tail, along the hips and backbone? It felt so good the way you massaged my muscles, it gave me great relief. I never showed you that I had any pain. I hid it well. After I passed, you told others I ran and played as if nothing was wrong, I didn't hinder my activities. This is true. I played hard, left nothing out, no holding back. I didn't want to worry anyone. I wanted to be pure joy, happiness and excitement.

"Michael believes the car accident caused this, it didn't. This was meant to be. Just like your lives are a journey, so are ours. We come to families for certain reasons. Just as Two-Bitts was Robynn's dog in childhood, **I WAS MAX**, Michael's dog before you both met. I, too, wanted to spend time with him once again, as our time together before was not finished. When our journeys are completed, it is our time to go, just like yours. Sometimes we are here to help a family or just a person. Sometimes we are here to help a cause, to bring awareness. We offer ourselves to be teachers, to change lives and to assist humans in their journeys.

"It is true we are ENERGY, pure energy. We are always accessible, just like now. And yes, this is me speaking, you are not thinking these words on your own. I know you are still shaking from the news that I was Max. You were so emotional and had to stop writing for a moment to gasp for breath. That's okay, I'm not going anywhere. I'll stay until we finish this chapter.

"Yes, at the clinic we saw into each others' souls. It is natural for you. You needed to experience this to confirm it was true. You have seen into the souls of other animals before, and you saw into mine. It was acceptance, not fear.

"You gave me comfort, peace and the family's presence. Everyone was comforting. But I was not to stay. You made the right decision. I know this has been weighing on your mind. You even listened to a spirit guide later to be sure. The guide confirmed as I left my body the energy was like the colors of the rainbow, twisting and folding like a ribbon in the wind, like a kite flying free. I was freed, freed from pain, finished with my journey and helping a family deal with separation. You said your goodbyes when you left for your trip, just like you always do, expecting to return to the way things always were. WE MUST REMEMBER TO NOT BE IN A HURRY WHEN WE SAY GOODBYE TO OTHERS, not that you need to have long goodbyes, rather be sure it is meaningful, just in case there is a moment when things aren't the same when you return.

"The energy work you shared in the clinic room was very pleasing, relieved the pain and provided comfort for my nearing end. This provided an opportunity for Michael to express his trust and confidence in your healing gifts and that he wanted this for me. I accepted your gifts, and the time you took to communicate with me, to reassure me of the love and happiness I gave you, was part of my journey.

"My message is the same as all in the animal kingdom: WE ARE PURE LOVE. Treat us with love, allow us to be, to do our jobs, as we all are here to do a certain task. Believe that we can communicate. Believe that we are energy and here to make a difference. Even after we leave, we can still be of assistance, just as you are witnessing now in this writing. As with Opal, 021, Jack, Pepper, Two-Bitts and many others, we can be heard. Anyone can hear us, they just have to train themselves to be still, be quiet, and connect with the energy of the Universe. There is much to learn from the animal kingdom. Size and species doesn't matter. We all have a journey and a purpose, too.

"May this chapter, although the last in your book, be the beginning of the difference in someone's life or the life of another animal." -- From me with love, Reggie

ABOUT THE AUTHOR

Robynn McCann

Most authors tell how many children they have, where they live and how many books they have written. Well, this is my first book so I don't have a long list of other titles, awards and certificates.

This book has been written from personal experience. I did not set out in life to be an author. I am formally educated in business/finance, which has been my support and focus for the past twenty-some years. Through the years I have realized that others, like myself, have come to a point in our lives where we are seeking out other opportunities, other interests different from where we started. It usually takes some event to cause the change.

In my case, it was moving to the country where the children could have farm animals that changed my focus. Sure, I still continued my current career and chosen path, but this major move set the scene and atmosphere for a new journey. It afforded me the opportunity to open up to my spiritual side, to expand my vision and knowledge of universal power and assistance.

It was during this time that I enrolled in animal communication courses, became certified in Reiki therapy and educated myself in color therapy, natural herbal remedies and other related subject matters. I have volunteered the last eight years, and still continue to volunteer, at a local animal refuge, where my contribution is to feed and care for mountain lions, wolves, coyotes, bears, a variety of monkeys, birds of prey and other wildlife.

This was not the first time in my life I touched my spiritual side; however, it was through the farm animals, their willingness to teach, willingness to sacrifice, that my shift in focus was more consistent, and that consistency produced this book.